# The Lady Lever Art Gallery

**Luke Fildes**
*William Hesketh Lever,* 1897
(Lady Lever Art Gallery, LL 3621; presented by the 3rd Viscount Leverhulme, 1980)

# The Lady Lever Art Gallery

## Port Sunlight

Published by:
The Bluecoat Press
Bluecoat Chambers
School Lane
Liverpool L1 3BX

ISBN 0 906367 84 0

Page make-up and typesetting by:
March Design,
Liverpool

Printed in Spain by GZ Printek
48170 Zamudio

Front cover illustration:
Edward John Gregory,
*Boulter's Lock, Sunday Afternoon*, 1882-97

**Notes**
Except where otherwise specified, dimensions are given in order of height, width and (for three-dimensional objects) depth.
For paintings, drawings and sculpture the nationality refers to the artist's place of birth. For all other objects the nationality refers to the place of manufacture. No nationality is cited for Wedgwood and Chinese Art, where it is self-evident.

# Contents

# Foreword

This new all-colour souvenir guidebook to the Lady Lever Art Gallery replaces the more modest black and white guide first published in 1984. Since then the Lady Lever Art Gallery, originally run by a charitable trust, has passed from the stewardship of the Merseyside County Council, which assumed responsibility in 1978, to that of the National Museums & Galleries on Merseyside, which took over in 1986. National status, granted in recognition of the outstanding quality of the collections, has enabled the Trustees of NMGM to make significant improvements to the Lady Lever Art Gallery, including the conversion of part of the basement to form a new café and shop, the installation of a lift and level access for visitors in wheelchairs, the publication of scholarly catalogues, and a new display devoted to the founder and the making of the Gallery.

William Hesketh Lever, later the 1st Viscount Leverhulme, established the Gallery in his factory village of Port Sunlight, as a cultural and educational resource for his workforce and the public at large. He did so because of his conviction that the study of art improved and refined the life of the individual. This belief is shared by the Trustees of NMGM. We hope this guidebook will further these ends by encouraging our many visitors to understand and enjoy the collections.

We would like to thank all those who have contributed to the guidebook: Xanthe Brooke, Robin Emmerson, Alex Kidson, Edward Morris, Andrew Renton and Lucy Wood for writing the text, David Flower and Colin Jackson for photography, Mike March for design work, Colin Wilkinson for seeing the book through the press, and above all, Lucy Wood for co-ordinating the project.

We are fortunate that the present Lord Leverhulme takes such an active and positive interest in the art gallery founded by his grandfather. The Trustees of NMGM greatly value the association between the family and this most personal and individual of galleries. We would like to thank him for his continuing and generous support.

Richard Foster
Director

Julian Treuherz
Keeper of Art Galleries

# The Creation of the Lady Lever Art Gallery

The Lady Lever Art Gallery – both the building and its collections – was the creation of one man, William Hesketh Lever, 1st Viscount Leverhulme (1851–1925), founder of Lever Brothers and the model village of Port Sunlight, and art collector on a scale unmatched in Britain since his death.

William Lever (hereafter 'Lever') was born in Bolton, Lancashire, the son of a wholesale grocer. The family were Congregationalists, and the nonconformist ethos of self-discipline and entrepreneurship was profoundly influential on Lever's whole life and career. He left school to join the family firm at the age of sixteen, becoming a salaried partner at 21, and devoted his energies to expanding the business in the 1870s and early '80s. It was only in 1884 that he decided to focus on selling a single product, household soap, to which he was drawn not by any technical interest in its manufacture – indeed at this stage the actual production was contracted out – but by its potential for marketing in pre-wrapped bars under a brand name. (Until then soap had been sold like cheese, cut to order for each customer from a large block.) Two years later he began to manufacture soap himself and established the new firm of Lever Brothers for the purpose, his brother and nominal partner James Darcy Lever being a semi-invalid who played little part in the business. Initially Lever took over an existing soap works in Warrington, but by 1888 he had outgrown the factory's capacity, and decided to build anew on a much larger scale. He chose a greenfield site on the Wirral shore of the Mersey, to build not only the factory but the adjacent village to house his employees – and named the whole complex Port Sunlight after his most successful brand of soap.

Lever's career as a serious collector also stems from this moment. In the late 1880s he began to buy pictures from the summer exhibitions of the Royal Academy, specifically for the purpose of advertising Sunlight Soap. His advertisement reproducing W.P. Frith's *New Frock*, bought at the 1889 summer exhibition, involved him in a notorious argument with the artist about the ethics of this use (or abuse) of art (Fig. 7). It also marked Lever's entrée into the London art market. At the same time his acquisition in 1888 of Thornton Manor, which he immediately set about enlarging, created opportunities for display on a larger stage than any of his previous houses had allowed. He himself always pointed to a pair of Derby biscuit porcelain figures (Fig. 1), acquired in the late 1870s for his house in Wigan, as the starting point of his collections, but it was the Port Sunlight venture that opened up grander possibilities of buying works of art, and it was only in the mid-1890s that Lever began collecting on a significant scale (Figs. 2 and 6).

Lever's metamorphosis from a casual art buyer to a serious collector was accelerated by his encounter, in or before 1896, with James Orrock (1829–1913), artist, collector and part-time dealer, and a passionate advocate of the merits of British art. Orrock had trained as a surgeon-dentist in Edinburgh, and practised

Fig. 1 Lever's house in Wigan, *c*.1877–80. On the chimneypiece is the pair of Derby biscuit figures that he regarded as the foundation-pieces of his art collection.

for some years in Nottingham before moving to London in about 1866 to become a full-time artist. He began buying works of art while in Nottingham, but in London he became a major collector, primarily of English 18th- and early 19th-century pictures and watercolours, of 18th-century English furniture and of 17th- and 18th-century Chinese porcelain (which he evidently regarded as an integral aspect of English baroque and Georgian taste). At the same time he campaigned vociferously for the establishment of a national gallery of British art – both fine and decorative – which he considered grossly neglected by the artistic establishment of his day.

Lever now took up Orrock's cause, and began to collect in a much more focused way, espousing the same periods as Orrock in English, and Chinese, art; and he bought Orrock's own collection in its entirety on three occasions, in 1904, 1910 and 1912. But he rapidly outstripped Orrock as a collector, in terms both of the quality and quantity of his collections, and of the scope of his interests. As a collector of 18th-century British portraits and landscapes – of which only a small proportion came to the Lady Lever Art Gallery – Lever was rivalled only by the great American collectors such as Henry Huntington and J. Pierpont Morgan; and in his purchase of English 17th- and 18th-century furniture he remains unequalled by any other private collector.

In addition Lever became an important collector of Victorian pictures, especially by the Pre-Raphaelites and their successors and by 'classical' artists such as Leighton and Alma-Tadema, his earliest acquisitions in this field (in 1893–4) probably predating his acquaintance with Orrock. He was also an early and prominent collector and patron of such sculptors as Edward Onslow Ford and Francis Derwent Wood, adherents of the anti-classical 'New Sculpture' movement. And in about 1900 he began to collect English 17th- and 18th-century embroideries, one of the first generation of British and American collectors to take an interest in this subject.

Fig. 2 The Adam Room at Thornton Manor, *c.*1898. (Unilever House Information Library, Blackfriars, London)

His collecting of Wedgwood began with the acquisition in 1905 of the highly distinguished collection formed by the 1st Lord Tweedmouth (1820–1894). Lever often bought in bulk from established collections – starting with his first block-purchase from Orrock in 1904 – to enhance both the size and the stature of his own collection. Thus his extensive purchases at the 1917 sale of Greek vases and Roman sculpture originally assembled by Thomas Hope (1769–1831) turned Lever's moderate holdings in this area into a major collection of antiquities. He made similar large-scale, and in some instances wholesale, purchases to build up his holdings of Chinese art and parts of his 'Museum' collection (see below).

Lever began to place parts of his collection on public display in some of the buildings of Port Sunlight from about 1902; and in the same year he opened Hall-i'-th'-Wood, a timber-framed house near his home town of Bolton, as a folk-museum, furnished with 16th- and 17th-century oak furniture. His private, and at that point more prestigious, collection also gained wider publicity after his purchase in 1904 of a house in Hampstead, The Hill, to which he at once decanted the majority of the works of art then at Thornton Manor. Two years later his company suffered commercial reverses which drastically reduced his purchasing power. But on his recovery around 1911 Lever was more than ever committed to public display of his collections: in that year he opened two museums: Rivington Hall, a largely 18th-century house on his Rivington estate in Lancashire; and Hulme Hall in Port Sunlight, originally built as the women employees' canteen but now adapted as a museum and art gallery and filled chiefly with the collections recently bought from Orrock.

The limitations of Hulme Hall as an art gallery were shown up by Lever's purchase in 1913 of a number of grand Victorian pictures at the sale of George McCulloch's collection, including Leighton's vast *Daphnephoria*. This was evidently the final catalyst to Lever's decision to establish a new, purpose-built public gallery in Port Sunlight Village, suitable for the display of these imposing works; the *Daphnephoria* itself still dominates the north end of the main hall for

Fig. 3 The Main Hall of the Lady Lever Art Gallery, *c*.1922

which it was always intended (Fig. 3). The first plans for the Gallery were laid in June 1913, and after his wife's death the following month Lever decided to name the Gallery in her memory. (He paid her another tribute when he was made a peer four years later by adding her maiden name of Hulme to his own surname to form his title; at her death he was already a baronet, so she was Lady Lever but never became Lady Leverhulme.)

Lever's architects were the Warrington firm of William & Segar Owen – who had been involved from the outset in the creation of Port Sunlight Village – but Lever himself exercised close control over every aspect of the building. It is in the classical style fostered by the Paris Ecole des Beaux Arts, a striking contrast to the English vernacular idiom of the Village housing; but it is likely that American architecture (on which Beaux Arts classicism was a powerful influence) provided the direct inspiration for Lever's choice. Beneath the Portland stone cladding, and the interior plasterwork, the Gallery is constructed of reinforced concrete, an early example of the use of this new material for a prominent building in Britain.

As with the building, so with its contents: Lever personally selected every work of art from his private collection that was to come to the Gallery. But its foundation also influenced his pattern of buying, for he now began to acquire pictures and objects specifically for display in the projected Gallery, which he might have passed by on his personal account. Although he had probably thought of founding a public art gallery from an early date (perhaps soon after taking up Orrock's campaign on behalf of British art), this conscious separation of his private and public collections marks a new departure. Partly it was simply a matter of scale: just as he had no room in his houses to do justice to the McCulloch collection, so he never intended the great state bed from Stowe (p. 50), bought in 1921, to be seen anywhere other than the Gallery. Partly, Lever had an

Fig. 4 The opening ceremony at the Lady Lever Art Gallery, 16 December 1922. Princess Beatrice is opening the south door, with Lever (hat in hand) behind. (Unilever Information Services, Port Sunlight Heritage Centre)

eye on the need to appeal to a wide public audience: thus he bought part of Sir Herbert Graystone's collection of armour in 1923, explaining to one of his dealers, 'I wanted these more as an attraction for those at the Gallery who ... do not particularly admire pictures, statuary, etc. I have to cater for all tastes at the Gallery.' More significantly, he weighted his selection of pictures in favour of Victorian works, especially narrative subjects, with much less emphasis on 18th-century painting than in his private collection: his instinct that the former would have more popular appeal has proved justified to this day.

However, Lever was also concerned to make his public collection more representative, perhaps seeking variety for its own sake, but also aiming to give a more informative picture of developments in certain key areas: thus he acquired some Elizabethan and Jacobean furniture, to complement the much more numerous later Stuart and Georgian pieces; he added Chinese hardstones and cloisonné enamels to his very large collection of Chinese porcelain; and he bought Greek and Roman antiquities presumably to underpin the classical basis of the collection as a whole.

The growth of the collections of fine and decorative art took place at the expense of Lever's so-called 'Museum' collection, which had been an important element in his original conception of the Gallery. Its nucleus, consisting mainly of ethnographic items, had been publicly displayed in Port Sunlight since at least 1903. Later additions to the 'Museum' section included most of the Greek and Roman antiquities and a collection of objects associated with Freemasonry, all of

Fig. 5 Lever lying in state in the Main Hall of the Gallery, beneath Leighton's *Daphnephoria*, 1925. (Unilever Information Services, Port Sunlight Heritage Centre)

which were bought specifically for the Gallery; but in the event the 'Art' collection expanded to fill the available gallery space, leaving little room for any 'Museum' material (with the exception of some antique sculpture). Much of it is now, however, exhibited in the William Hesketh Lever Display, which was opened in 1996 in order, partly, to honour the founder's original intentions for the display of this collection.

The Lady Lever Art Gallery was eventually opened in 1922 by Princess Beatrice (youngest daughter of Queen Victoria), progress having been delayed by the First World War (Fig. 4); but even after this Lever continued adding to the collection for the remaining three years of his life. After his death in May 1925 the parts of his collection that had not been selected for the Gallery (approximately half) were dispersed in a series of sales, lasting altogether forty-five days, in both London and New York. But despite the fact that Lever was still sorting his private collection from this public bequest when he died, the best of his extraordinary accumulation of works of art had already been placed in the Gallery. It remains, notwithstanding the dedication to his wife, a remarkable memorial to *his* taste and philanthropy.

# chapter 1

# Paintings and Sculpture

By the time of his death in 1925, Lord Leverhulme owned thousands of paintings, drawings and sculptures. The vast majority of these works were British, reflecting his long-held wish to create, in the shape of the Lady Lever Art Gallery, a public gallery of British art that would present a more rounded picture of the achievements of the national school than could be found in any existing institution at that date. The precise flavour of the gallery, in which fine and decorative arts would be displayed together, and in which a select group of foreign works would contrast with and set off the 'national' characteristics of the bulk of the contents, closely reflected the views and tastes of Lever's friend James Orrock, the collector and dealer who, on three occasions between 1904 and his death in 1913, sold Lever his own collections in their entirety. The strengths (and weaknesses) in the Gallery's late 18th- and early 19th-century British holdings in particular are a testimony to his influence.

By the canons of his time, Lever's British pictures offered a rich and representative survey of the greatness of the national school. The collection did not entirely neglect 17th- and early 18th-century art, but it concentrated heavily on the period from about 1750 to 1900 when British painting was widely perceived to have reached and indeed exceeded in stature that of other European countries. Within that period, Lever concentrated further on three areas where such claims might carry particular weight. The first featured the foundation and rise of the Royal Academy. Concentrating on the grand-manner portraiture of Sir Joshua Reynolds and the Italian landscapes of Richard Wilson, Lever built up a core of paintings that witnessed British artists, while sustaining the favourite national genres of the portrait and the landscape, for the first time engaging maturely with the mainstream classical tradition of European art. This cluster of works, whose highlights are Reynolds's *Duchess of Hamilton* and Wilson's *Landscape with Diana and Callisto*, both from the end of the 1750s, was set in relief by a series of less imposing, but at the time equally fashionable, Georgian pictures: chiefly portraits by Gainsborough, Romney and Hoppner, and the rustic scenes of Morland and Wheatley. (By contrast, the group of four enamel paintings by George Stubbs, which from today's vantage point are much the most remarkable early British pictures in the collection, probably appealed to Lever largely as unusual examples of Wedgwood ware.)

The second area very fully represented in Lever's collection was the golden age of British landscape painting, roughly from 1800 to 1850. Constable and Turner, with their altogether new intensity of response to the landscape and the forces of nature, were then as now regarded as the dominant figures of this era; but almost equally significant for Lever were the landscapists whose greatest contribution had been in the medium of watercolour. James Orrock, himself an accomplished watercolourist, was a proponent of the since widely-held view that perfecting the watercolour was the British School's most significant contribution to the history of Western art, and he sold Lever many examples by a canon of key figures, notably David Cox, Peter de Wint, William Henry Hunt and George Barret junior.

Fig. 6 The Music Room at Thornton Manor, *c*.1903. Among the pictures hanging on the end wall are Millais's *Black Brunswickers*, Leighton's *Fatidica*, and *Napoleon Reading his Letter of Abdication* by George Richmond; on the left wall hangs Romney's *Mrs Oliver*, flanked by two Hoppner portraits, *The Earl of Moira* and *Lady Elizabeth Howard* (see p. 23). All of these are now in the Lady Lever Art Gallery. (RCHME © Crown Copyright)

A contemporary of these artists, working in a very different tradition, was William Etty, a favourite artist of Orrock and Lever alike. Etty's mastery as a colourist, and the decorative properties of his rich canvases, were probably the main attraction for both of them; but Lever's taste for Etty is suggestive in further ways. On the one hand, as his collection of later 19th-century paintings and more especially sculpture indicates, Lever was very far from shy of the nude figure (the mastery of which lay at the heart of all Academic art). On the other, Etty seems to have answered in Lever an almost compulsive collector's urge in some sense to corner a particular supply: an impulse recognizable in his approach to a number of other artists, which seems intimately bound up with his instincts as a manufacturer and businessman.

The third key area, which dominates the collection, was Victorian art. It was in this field that Lever first began to collect seriously, independently of Orrock's influence, and he continued to do so even after developing other interests. In the late 1880s he started acquiring contemporary, and relatively minor, British paintings for use in advertisements for Sunlight Soap (Fig. 7), which explains the number of girls in white frocks, salubrious family gatherings and scenes featuring washing and bathing still to be found in the Gallery. But by the early 1890s he was buying the work of Frederic Leighton and, a little later, of J.E. Millais, who together with Etty remained his favourite artists throughout his life.

Many of Lever's most important Victorian pictures came from the Christie's sale in 1913 of the collection of George McCulloch (1848–1907), the greatest single private collection of Victorian and Edwardian paintings ever formed. Born in Glasgow, McCulloch made his fortune in Australia, where he emigrated in 1883 to run a sheep-farming station, but discovered and exploited a silver mine at Broken Hill, the immense success of which enabled him to start collecting. In 1892 he returned to live in London, and a few years later built himself a new house in Queen's Gate to accommodate his expanding collection. At his

Fig. 7 Lever's advertisement for Sunlight Soap using Frith's *New Frock*. (Unilever Information Services, Port Sunlight Heritage Centre.)

posthumous sale of 1913, Lever was by far the most notable buyer, securing Leighton's *Daphnephoria* and *Garden of the Hesperides*, Millais's *Sir Isumbras at the Ford* and *Lingering Autumn*, as well as major works by lesser artists, such as Luke Fildes, Henry Moore and J.M. Swan; and it is no coincidence that he decided to commission the Lady Lever Art Gallery only a few weeks afterwards.

Until the McCulloch sale the majority of Lever's Victorian acquisitions had been contemporary or near-contemporary works: a policy he continued with, for example, the acquisition of two important late works by J.W. Waterhouse in 1916 and 1917. But after the Gallery's inception he concentrated mainly on assembling a representative collection of mid- and late Victorian art. The major figures of the Pre-Raphaelite movement are all present: Holman Hunt's uncompromisingly realistic masterpieces, *The Scapegoat* and *May Morning on Magdalen Tower*, contrasting with the more 'aesthetic' works of Rossetti and his younger associate Burne-Jones. Social realism is represented by Herkomer's *The Last Muster*, while Orchardson's *The Young Duke* and *St Helena 1816: Napoleon dictating his memoirs to Count Las Cases* are major examples of late Victorian historical drama. Lever also selected a few works by his friends: landscapes by Alfred East and David Murray, and Luke Fildes's *Al-fresco Toilette*, perhaps the grandest scene from everyday Venetian life in late Victorian art.

Lever's taste in sculpture was more progressive: personal friendships – with Onslow Ford and Goscombe John – probably played a larger part and he became the single most important patron of the 'New Sculpture'. This movement brought a new poetic realism into British sculpture with a wider range of techniques, of subject- matter and of pose, and its highly imaginative bronzes complement the mythic masterpieces of Burne-Jones, Rossetti, Waterhouse and Leighton. Lever's deep commitment to 18th-century classicism and especially to Victorian high art makes the Lady Lever Art Gallery one of the most outstanding and distinctive displays of British paintings and sculpture ever assembled by a single collector.

**Spanish (Valencia)**
*St. Ursula before the King of the Huns, c.*1400–10
Tempera on panel;
116.5 x 64 cm
Purchased by Lever, 1919;
inv. no. LL 3428 (WHL 3752c)

One of four panels from the lower half of an altarpiece illustrating the story of the martyrdom of St. Ursula and her 11,000 female followers, who were massacred by the King of the Huns at Cologne. The four upper panels are in the Prado Museum, Madrid, and all originally came from an altarpiece in the Dominican church of San Pablo in Palencia, Castile. It was probably the highly decorative nature of the paintings, with their skilled use of punched work and tooling on the gold background and the wealth of detail in the dress, textiles and patterned flooring, that attracted Lever to these panels, unusual in his collection for being foreign and medieval.

**Richard Wilson**
**(1713–1782)**
British (Welsh)
*Diana and Callisto, c.*1757
Oil on canvas; 103 x 139 cm
Purchased by Lever, 1904;
inv. no. LL 3122 (WHL 641)

The painting, one of several known versions of the subject by Wilson, may have been executed during the artist's stay in Italy between 1752 and 1757. It would have been intended for purchase by an aristocratic collector making the Grand Tour. It is a view of Lake Nemi, a beauty spot not far from Rome and a site familiar to readers of the classics for its association with the goddess Diana. The lake was known as Diana's mirror and there was a shrine to her in the groves above the shore. Wilson alludes to this by representing in the foreground the story of Diana and Callisto from Ovid's *Metamorphoses*. The goddess has just discovered her handmaiden's pregnancy and is banishing her: Callisto's child will be the forefather of the Arcadian people. The calm lucidity and order of Wilson's design consciously recall French classical landscapes of the 17th century by Gaspar Dughet and Claude Lorrain.

**Perino del Vaga (1501–1547)**
Italian
*The Trojans appear before Dido, c.*1536–9
Ink and wash with white highlights on
grey washed paper; 23.6 x 18.1 cm
Purchased by Lever from the
Earl of Pembroke's sale, 1917;
inv. no. LL 3044 (WHL 3288)

In the foreground the shipwrecked Trojan companions of Aeneas explain their plight to the enthroned Queen Dido, whose attention has been attracted by the cloud which veils Aeneas from her sight. The drawing is possibly a second design for a tapestry illustrating the scene, which was commissioned by Andrea Doria, the Genoese military commander (and is now in the Royal Palace, Madrid).

**Giovacchino Fortini (1671–1736)**
Italian (Florence)
*Bust of Ferdinando de' Medici, c.*1700
Marble;
139 (including base) x 90.3 x 59.5 cm
Purchased by Lever, 1922;
inv. no. LL 203 (X 4168)

Prince Ferdinando de' Medici of Tuscany (1633–1713) was a great patron of the arts in Florence, with a particular fondness for sculpture. His emblem, lightning striking through clouds, has been carved into his breastplate in the form of a shield, and the related motto, ET LUCET ET TERRET ('It casts both light and terror'), is on the base. Fortini was known for his tomb and church sculpture as well as being an accomplished sculptor of portrait busts and medals, and paid subtle attention to finely worked detail and textural distinctions.

**Sir Joshua Reynolds
(1723–1792)**
British
*Elizabeth Gunning, Duchess of
Hamilton and Duchess of
Argyll*, 1760
Oil on canvas;
238.5 x 147.5 cm
Purchased by Lever from
the Hamilton Palace sale,
1919;
inv. no. LL 3126 (WHL 4093)

One of Reynolds's greatest
essays in the grand manner,
this portrait was shown at
the first-ever Society of
Artists exhibition held in
London in 1760. It was
clearly intended to display
his powers and his theory of
portraiture. The sitter, a
famous Irish beauty, had
married the 6th Duke of
Hamilton in 1752; recently
widowed at the time of this
portrait, she was shortly to
marry John Campbell, the
future 5th Duke of Argyll.
Reynolds portrays her in
peeress's robes, but the rest
of her costume and her
features are idealized,
giving her something of the
air of an antique sculpture.
The doves and the relief
sculpture of the Judgement
of Paris on the left are
allusions to the goddess
Venus, and are devices
typical of Reynolds's
intellectual and elevated
brand of portraiture.

**Sir Joshua Reynolds
(1723–1792)**
British
*Mrs Peter Beckford*, 1782
Oil on canvas; 239 x 147 cm
Purchased by Lever from
the Hamilton Palace sale,
1919;
inv no. LL 3125 (WHL 4094)

This full-length portrait is
characteristic of the works
by which Reynolds
represented himself, as its
President, in the Royal
Academy's exhibitions of
the 1780s. The sitter, wife of
a Dorset gentleman, was of a
delicate constitution and
Reynolds portrays her
making a libation (a drink-
offering) to the Greek
goddess of health, Hygeia,
whose emblem was a snake.
At the time the portrait was
painted Louisa Beckford
was in the throes of an affair
with her husband's
celebrated cousin William
Beckford, author of the
famous Gothic novel *Vathek*;
and Reynolds's conception,
with its gloomy, smoke-
filled atmosphere and
elaborate play of light and
shadow, may owe
something to Beckford's
newly-fashionable literary
and aesthetic image.

**Thomas Gainsborough
(1727–1788)**
British
*Anne Duchess of Cumberland, c.1780*
Oil on canvas; 76.5 x 63.5 cm
Purchased by Lever, 1920;
inv. no. LL 3140 (WHL 4242)

Lever bought this fine example of
Gainsborough's later manner as a portrait of
Princess Augusta, daughter of George III. She,
however, was only a girl when most of
Gainsborough's portraits of the Royal Family
were undertaken, and the sitter's features
strongly resemble those of Anne Duchess of
Cumberland, a previously-married commoner
who controversially became the wife of the
King's brother in 1771. Horace Walpole
described her 'with eyelashes a yard long, a
coquette beyond measure and as artful as
Cleopatra'. Gainsborough painted her, always
sympathetically, on several occasions, and this
work combines brilliance with intimacy and
tenderness.

**Johann Zoffany (1734/5–1810)**
German
*Robert Baddeley as Moses in Sheridan's 'The School
for Scandal',* 1781
Oil on canvas; 76.5 x 61 cm
Purchased by the Trustees of the Lady Lever Art
Gallery, 1930; inv. no. LL 3535 (LP 32)

The son of a Frankfurt cabinet-maker, Zoffany
trained in Germany and Italy, but from 1760
made his career mainly in London. Together
with groups and conversation pieces, theatrical
portraits were a speciality of his. They were a
form of publicity for celebrated actors who were
usually shown at climactic moments of their
best-known roles. Baddeley took the role of
Moses when 'The School for Scandal' was first
performed at Drury Lane Theatre in 1777, and is
here shown in the scene in which he buys Sir
Charles Surface's family portraits.
Characteristically, the illusion of a staged
performance is played down and the action
presented as though it were happening in real
life. The painting was one of those purchased by
Lever's Trustees after his death in order to round
out the Gallery's historic British collections.

**George Romney (1734–1802)**
British
*Sarah Rodbard*, 1784
Oil on canvas; 236 x 152 cm
Purchased by Lever, 1903;
inv. no. LL 3539 (WHL 50)

In 1784, when he painted this outstanding full-length,
Romney was London's most fashionable portrait
painter. He avoided the formality and intellectual
pretension of his rival, Sir Joshua Reynolds, in favour
of a mood of relaxed elegance, which he achieved
through assured, flowing draughtsmanship and
restrained colour. Sarah Rodbard was nineteen at the
time of the portrait; two years later she became the
wife of Major (later General Sir Eyre) Coote. Lever's
purchase of this work for the high price of £12,000
assured him celebrity status as a collector of Georgian
portraiture.

**John Hoppner (1758–1810)**
British
*Lady Elizabeth Howard,*
*later Duchess of Rutland*, 1798
Oil on canvas; 127 x 101.5 cm
Purchased by Lever, 1897;
inv. no. LL 3128 (WHL 73)

The sitter, eighteen years old at the date of this
portrait, was the daughter of Frederick, 5th Earl of
Carlisle, a member of the Whig aristocracy in the circle
of the Prince Regent. Through the influence of this
group of patrons, Hoppner established himself as a
natural successor to Sir Joshua Reynolds in the 1790s,
developing Reynolds's manner, with its concentration
on warm, harmonious colour, tonal subtlety and a
richly-worked surface. Although less brilliant and
adventurous than his great rival Lawrence, Hoppner
at his best – as here – achieved portraits of genuine
poetry and feeling.

**John Flaxman (1755–1826)**
British
*Cephalus and Aurora*, 1790
Marble; 146 x 102 x 67 cm
Purchased by Lever at the
Hope Heirlooms sale, 1917;
presented to the Gallery by
the 2nd Viscount
Leverhulme, 1929;
inv. no. LL 713 (LS 5)

The story of Cephalus, retold in Ovid's *Metamorphoses*, was popular among artists in the 17th and 18th centuries. Flaxman represents the moment in which the youth, after resisting her advances, finally yields to the amorous Aurora, Greek goddess of the dawn. It was one of the artist's first major sculptures and was made in Rome, where he had travelled to study the antique: a trip financed by his work for Josiah Wedgwood. The sculpture was a commission from the celebrated collector Thomas Hope, one of the prime movers of neo-classical taste; it formed the centrepiece of the famous 'Star Room' (decorated throughout with emblems of dawn and the retreating night) at Hope's London house in Duchess Street. Lever purchased it with many of his antique sculptures at the Hope Heirlooms Sale.

**George Stubbs (1724–1806)**
British
*Self-Portrait*, 1782
Enamel on Wedgwood
earthenware plaque; 93 x 71 cm
Purchased by Lever from the
Tweedmouth collection, 1905;
inv. no. LL 3684 (H 374)

This is one of a handful of
surviving enamels which Stubbs
painted on ceramic plaques
manufactured by Josiah
Wedgwood. Stubbs devoted
considerable energy to
experimenting with and gradually
perfecting this new medium, which
he believed to be more durable
than oil painting on canvas. He
exhibited a group of enamels, of
which this was one, at the Royal
Academy in 1782; but other artists
did not respond to them as
enthusiastically as both he and
Wedgwood had hoped. Acquired
almost incidentally as part of Lord
Tweedmouth's Wedgwood
collection (see p. 72), this oval was
perhaps Lever's most remarkable
single purchase of an 18th-century
British painting. To complement it
he later bought its three
companions now in the Gallery.

**George Stubbs (1724–1806)**
British
*Haycarting*, 1795
Enamel on Wedgwood earthenware
plaque; 77 x 105 cm
Purchased by Lever, 1915;
inv. no. LL 3683 (WHL 2180)

One of three enamels which Stubbs
executed in the mid-1790s on the
theme of haymaking. Although they
are repetitions, with slight
variations, of subjects which he had
painted in oils over a decade
previously, they can be seen as the
apogee of his work in enamel,
limpid in colour and masterly in
design. The figures, carefully
studied in relation to each other,
have a statuesque, arresting quality
which elevates them from the type
of common rural labourer into the
individual heroes of some frieze
from antiquity.

**Joseph Mallord William Turner (1775–1851)**
British
*The Falls of the Clyde, c.*1840
Oil on canvas; 89 x 119.5 cm
Purchased by Lever, 1923;
inv. no. LL 3584 (WHL 4708)

One of a group of late and experimental oils, not intended for public exhibition, in which Turner freely reworked subjects he had first treated decades before. The source for this canvas was a large watercolour he had completed in 1802, now in the Walker Art Gallery, Liverpool. Situated on the upper Clyde near Lanark, the falls had become an attraction for tourists at the end of the 18th century when they had been painted by a number of artists. Turner's abiding fascination with the effects of strong light, here playing on the spray of cascading water, converts a picturesque scene into a profound expression of the elemental forces and primary colours of nature.

**Joseph Mallord William Turner (1775–1851)**
British
*Dudley, c.*1832
Watercolour and bodycolour on paper; 28 x 43 cm
Purchased by Lever, 1919; inv. no. LL 3923 (WHL 4030)

Turner's view incorporates both the antiquity of the hillside market town, with its castle and church, and the industrial life of a great new centre for the manufacture of glass and iron. The harsh glare of the forges and the brilliant light reflected in the water of the foreground canal impart a supernatural quality to this spectacular and sublime vision of the Industrial Revolution, suddenly erupting within England's ancient landscape. This watercolour, made for the series *Picturesque views in England and Wales*, shows Turner's ability to transform an ordinary landscape and everyday life into a splendid panorama of light and colour.

**John Constable (1776–1837)**
British
*Cottage at East Bergholt, c.1833*
Oil on canvas; 87.5 x 112 cm
Purchased by Lever, 1904;
inv. no. LL 3120 (WHL 557)

The strips of canvas added to both sides suggest that Constable made this sketch to work out the composition for a proposed exhibition picture. The title is an invention: though the scene is reminiscent of many of his Suffolk landscapes, and combines motifs from earlier paintings, the specific viewpoint has not been identified and may have been imaginary. At the time of its acquisition by Lever the work was notorious: the subject of a celebrated debate over Constable forgeries. Today it is prized as one of the artist's finest late works, a tour-de-force of palette-knife painting and an image of brooding, almost mystical power.

**William Etty (1787–1849)**
British
*The Judgement of Paris,* 1825–6
Oil on canvas; 183 x 277 cm
Purchased by Lever, 1911;
inv. no. LL 3588 (WHL 642)

Paris, the son of King Priam, hands the apple to Aphrodite, goddess of love, in preference to her rivals, and sets in train the events that will lead to the Trojan Wars. Etty, who excelled with subjects suited to the female nude, was one of the few British artists of the period to enjoy success as a history painter and this was one of his grandest works. It was commissioned by the 4th Earl of Darnley and exhibited at the Royal Academy in 1826. Etty's sources included the famous engraving of Raphael's *Judgement of Paris* by Marcantonio Raimondi and Flaxman's illustrations to the *Iliad,* but his rich colour is indebted to Venetian art, above all that of his mentor Titian.

**Sir John Everett Millais
(1829–1898)**
British
*A Dream of the Past: Sir
Isumbras at the Ford*, 1857
Oil on canvas; 125.5 x 171.5 cm
Purchased by Lever from the
George McCulloch sale, 1913;
inv. no. LL 3625 (WHL 19)

An example of the Pre-Raphaelites' interest in subjects about medieval chivalry: an ancient knight in golden armour is carrying the children of a poor woodcutter across a river. Sir Isumbras is a character from a 14th-century English romance, but this incident does not occur in the poem. It may have been invented by Millais's friend the art critic Tom Taylor, who wrote a fake medieval verse explaining the story. Many critics thought the horse was too big, and it was repainted several times, but the landscape background was much admired. Its loose and fluid handling, which contrasts with the artist's earlier more detailed landscape style, captures the fleeting effect of twilight, with a solemnity perhaps intended to suggest a deeper, spiritual meaning about the end of the knight's quest and the transience of worldly deeds.

**George Mason (1818–1872)**
British
*The Gander*, 1864–5
Oil on canvas; 48.5 x 83.6 cm
Purchased by Lever, 1920;
inv. no. LL 3146 (WHL 4112)

The artist has selected a very ordinary, even slightly humorous, subject – a peasant girl shooing away some angry geese. But he has treated it with such poetry and refinement that an everyday incident becomes high art. The long simple lines of the Staffordshire moors and hills, the grey twilight and the statuesque pose of the girl give to the scene a quiet grandeur and an emotional force remarkable for their intensity in such a reticent painting. Mason spent many years in Italy and even his English landscapes have a classical sense of structure and composition.

**Sir John Everett Millais (1829–1898)**
British
*Spring (Apple Blossoms)*, 1859
Oil on canvas; 110.5 x 45.7 cm
Purchased by Lever, 1920; purchased
from the 3rd Viscount Leverhulme for
the Lady Lever Art Gallery, 1986, with
the assistance of the National Heritage
Memorial Fund;
inv. no. LL 3624 (WHL 4114)

Though known for his historical narrative paintings such as *Sir Isumbras at the Ford* and *The Black Brunswickers*, Millais at about the same time painted a small number of modern dress pictures without specific stories. They were 'mood' pictures intended to awaken 'the deepest religious reflection', to quote the artist's own words. The girls, relaxing in an orchard of spring blossom, are tasting curds and cream, but the underlying theme is the transience of youth and beauty, expressed in the fragile bloom of adolescence, the wild flowers and the changing seasons; and the inevitability of death, whose presence is indicated by the scythe on the right. The type of picture, showing contemplative figures seated in an idyllic landscape, goes back to the *fête champêtre* paintings of Titian and Giorgione, and anticipates the figure compositions of dreamy young women painted by Whistler in the 1860s.

**Frederick Walker**
**(1840–1875)**
British
*The Bathers*, 1865–9
Oil on canvas; 92.7 x 214.7 cm
Purchased by Lever, 1918;
inv. no. LL 3143 (WHL 3420)

This painting seems to show just a few boys drying themselves after bathing in the Thames near Cookham where the artist painted his subject on the spot to ensure accuracy of tone and colour. In fact, Walker has borrowed many of his poses from famous Greek and Roman sculptures and his subject from a famous cartoon by Michelangelo, also called *The Bathers*, representing an incident from a battle. Some contemporary critics found the final result close to parody but the classical grandeur and grace achieved by Walker were a remarkable achievement for an artist not yet thirty years old.

**Ford Madox Brown (1821–1893)**
British
*Cromwell on his farm*, 1873–4
Oil on canvas; 143 x 104.3 cm
Purchased by Lever, 1899;
inv. no. LL 3641 (WHL 21)

The future Lord Protector is shown as a Huntingdonshire farmer before his rise to power during the English Civil Wars. Although everyday life on his farm teems obtrusively around him, Cromwell stares prophetically into the future. The symbolism is rich. Cromwell's oak sapling represents his future strength, while the bonfire demonstrates divine wrath at royalist England. Cromwell was one of the great leaders hero-worshipped by Thomas Carlyle, whose writings deeply influenced Brown and inspired this painting; both author and artist profoundly admired Cromwell's political and religious radicalism.

**William Holman Hunt
(1827–1910)**
British
*The Scapegoat*, 1854
Oil on canvas; 87 x 139.8 cm
Purchased by Lever, 1923;
inv. no. LL 3623 (WHL 4706)

Each year on the Day of Atonement, the High Priest in the Temple of Jerusalem cast a goat out into the desert as a symbolic act of expiation for the sins of the Israelites. The custom is described in the Old Testament, but Hunt linked it to the New Testament, making the animal into a symbol of Christ, who took upon himself the sins of the world: the scarlet thread around its horns, referred to in the Talmud, suggests the crown of thorns. The goat stares out accusingly, giving the picture an uncomfortable yet memorable emotional force. Hunt travelled to Palestine to search out authentic settings for his Biblical scenes, and this landscape was painted by the desolate shores of the Dead Sea, at a spot thought to be the site of the city of Sodom. The vivid colours and sharply painted details are characteristic of Pre-Raphaelite naturalism.

**Sir Hubert von Herkomer (1849–1914)**
British
*The Last Muster: Sunday at the Royal Hospital,
Chelsea,* 1875
Oil on canvas; 214.5 x 159 cm
Purchased by Lever, 1923;
inv. no. LL 3627 (WHL 4705)

Painted after the artist had attended a service at the
chapel of the Royal Hospital, Chelsea, a home for
veteran soldiers ('Chelsea Pensioners') who were
unable to support themselves after leaving the army.
Herkomer wrote, 'The idea was to make every man tell
some different story, to be told by his face, or by the
selection of attitude.' The attitude of the central figure,
slumped forward, his stick slipping from his grasp,
indicates that he has indeed answered 'the last
muster'; his neighbour anxiously feels his pulse.
Poverty and death were unusual subjects for Victorian
painters, who invariably presented them in an
ennobling and dignified light. Herkomer had made his
name with illustrations of social deprivation in the
*Graphic* magazine, and first published a version of this
subject in 1871. He then worked it up into this
painting, which received high praise at the Royal
Academy and went on to win a gold medal at the Paris
exhibition of 1878.

**William Holman Hunt (1827–1910)**
British
*May Morning on Magdalen Tower,* 1890
Oil on canvas; 154.5 x 200 cm
Purchased by Lever, 1919;
inv. no. LL 3599 (WHL 4042)

This shows the ceremony of greeting
the sun on May Morning from the top
of the tower of Magdalen College,
Oxford. Hunt's aim was to create a
modern religious subject, linking
contemporary Christian worship with
ancient times. The ceremony was
thought to originate with the Druids,
and the inclusion of a Parsee, an
Indian sun worshipper, from the
Indian Institute at Oxford, further
indicates the pantheistic tenor of
Hunt's symbolism, which associates
the light of the sun, spring flowers,
music and boyhood innocence with
the Divine force. Hunt also designed
the beaten copper frame (made by
C.R. Ashbee's Guild of Handicraft),
showing the sun awakening plants
and animals into life. The figures are
portraits of the President, Fellows and
choristers of the college, though some
of the boys were not members of the
choir but were included for their
looks: despite the convincing 'truth to
nature' of the scene, Hunt's purpose
was primarily symbolic, not realistic.

**Edward Coley Burne-Jones (1833–1898)**
British
*The Beguiling of Merlin*, 1872–7
Oil on canvas; 186 x 111 cm
Purchased by Lever, 1918;
inv. no. LL 3121 (WHL 3509)

The story is taken from the Arthurian Legends, which were the artist's favourite subjects. Merlin had fallen in love with Nimue (also called Nimiane, Vivian or Vivien). This enabled her to learn his skills in enchantment and here she is sending Merlin into a deep sleep. Burne-Jones had become infatuated with one of his admirers, Mary Zambaco, in the 1860s, and so the powerful sexual tension in the painting reflected his own situation. The long sinuous lines of her figure and of the hawthorn trees behind still entrance the spectator – as they bewitched Merlin in the legend.

**Dante Gabriel Rossetti (1826–1882)**
British
*The Blessed Damozel*, 1875–9
Oil on canvas; 111 x 82.7 cm,
plus predella 36.5 x 82.8 cm
Purchased by Lever, 1922;
inv. no. LL 3148 (WHL 4391)

This illustrates Rossetti's much earlier poem of about 1850 about a damsel who died young and went to heaven, where she pined for her earthbound lover, waiting for him to die so that they could be re-united. She is depicted as described in the poem's first stanza, leaning from the gold bar of Heaven: 'She had three lilies in her hand, and the stars in her hair were seven.'
Many of Rossetti's paintings of this period feature scenes of unhappy or unconsummated love. There is a larger version of this picture in the Fogg Art Museum, Harvard. Both use the format of a Renaissance altarpiece, with the main scene in a large panel and a smaller predella panel below for the secondary figure.

**Frederic Leighton (1830–1896)**
British
*The Daphnephoria*, 1874–6
Oil on canvas; 231 x 525 cm
Purchased by Lever from the George
McCulloch sale, 1913;
inv. no. LL 3632 (WHL 1177)

The Daphnephoria was an ancient festival held in honour of Apollo commemorating in particular a Theban victory over the Aeolians. This is the grandest of a group of huge processional pictures on which Leighton's reputation largely rests. His classical vision of the beauty of form, his skill in grouping and arranging his figures and his imagination in conceiving the rich and luxuriant setting make this one of the very few British paintings which can be compared with the great historical and mythological works of 19th-century France and Germany. It was painted for the dining room of his close friend and patron, the banker James Stewart Hodgson, who was compelled to sell it following the first collapse of Barings Bank in 1890.

**Frederic Leighton (1830–1896)**
British
*The Garden of the Hesperides*, 1891–2
Oil on canvas; 169.5 x 169.5 cm
Purchased by Lever from the
George McCulloch sale, 1913;
inv. no. LL 3139 (WHL 29)

The Hesperides, daughters of Hesperus, the god of evening, protected the golden apples given to Juno or Jupiter on their marriage. They were helped by the dragon, Ladon, who never slept. In due course Hercules killed the dragon and stole the apples but here the artist has selected an idyllic moment of perfect harmony as the Hesperides sing to the sleepless dragon. This harmony is also reflected in the composition of the painting with the long undulating lines of the figures, draperies and animals echoing the circular format of the picture. The flat almost abstract design and the static, emotionless figures are characteristic of many of the artist's late works.

33

**Lawrence Alma-Tadema
(1836–1912)**
Dutch
*The Tepidarium*, 1881
Oil on panel; 24 x 33 cm
Purchased by Lever from
A. and F. Pears Ltd., 1916;
inv. no. LL 3130 (WHL 2898)

Alma-Tadema was born in
Holland but settled in London,
where he achieved great success
with his scenes of daily life in
ancient times. The tepidarium
was the warm Roman bath; the
girl holds an ostrich feather and a
strigel used for scraping the skin
after soaping and oiling it. Alma-
Tadema generally contrasts
erudite archaeology with
aggressively modern figures and
attitudes. He was also the most
gifted exponent among Victorian
painters in rendering exactly
textures, surfaces and colours.
This combination of realism and
learning proved very
disconcerting when applied to the
nude, and it is surprising that A.
and F. Pears could ever have
considered using this painting in
a soap advertisement, appropriate
for the purpose as it is.

**Samuel Luke Fildes (1843–1927)**
British
*An Al-fresco Toilette*, 1887–9
Oil on canvas; 173 x 108 cm
Purchased by Lever from the
George McCulloch sale, 1913;
inv. no. LL 3621 (WHL 16)

The Neo-Venetian School was an international
group of artists painting an idealized version of the
everyday life of working-class inhabitants of Venice
in the 1880s and 1890s. Fildes briefly belonged to
this school before turning to portraiture around 1890
(see frontispiece). Here he has contrasted the
grandeur of 16th- and 17th-century Venetian palaces
with the frivolity of their late 19th-century tenants.
In fact, the palace was the studio of the artist's
brother-in-law and the models included his wife
and young son. The artificiality of the final result
may have suggested to the artist that he should seek
other subjects, although his command of grouping
and pose is remarkable.

**William Quiller Orchardson (1832–1910)**
British
*The Young Duke,* 1889
Oil on canvas; 147 x 252 cm
Purchased by Lever, 1916;
inv. no. LL 3612 (WHL 2872)

This is an imaginary scene set in early 18th-century France. Guests at a banquet are drinking a toast to the seated young duke who is celebrating his coming of age. The subtle and restrained colour harmonies, together with the immensely skilful still-life painting in the foreground, are remarkable technical achievements, largely reflecting the artist's Scottish training. Dissolute aristocratic life in the 18th century was a popular subject in 19th-century Britain, and the artist probably intended to contrast the splendour of the setting and of the occasion with the rather drunken appearance of the participants.

**William Powell Frith (1819–1909)**
British
*The New Frock,* 1889
Oil on canvas; 92 x 72 cm
Purchased by Lever from the artist, 1889;
presented to the Gallery by Lever Brothers, 1983;
inv. no. LL 3419

Lever first began to collect paintings in the late 1880s in order to acquire images that could be incorporated into advertisements for the Sunlight Soap manufactured by his company. In this painting, the sentimental emphasis on the girl's pride in her appearance and clothes made it ideal for the purpose, although the artist vigorously protested at what he saw as the prostitution of his art for commercial purposes (Fig. 7, see p. 16). He had in fact entitled the painting, 'Vanity of vanities, all is vanity', so his message was exactly the opposite to that insisted on by Lever in his soap advertisements.

**Edward John Gregory (1850–1909)**
British
*Boulter's Lock, Sunday Afternoon*, 1882–97
Oil on canvas; 215 x 142 cm
Purchased by Lever from the C.J. Galloway sale,
1905; inv. no. LL 3149 (WHL 33)

Boating on the upper Thames, particularly in the
picturesque sections of the river around
Maidenhead where this scene is located, was a
national pastime in the late 19th century. Gregory
has painted a panorama of upper middle-class
social life: the 'new' woman energetically paddling
her own canoe is contrasted with the young woman
in the foreground with her lap dog delicately
holding the tasselled steering ropes; the artist
himself lies back watching the scene at the extreme
right, while the other men struggle to get their boats
out of the lock. The very high view-point and the
manner in which boats are cut off by the edge of the
painting reflect 'advanced' theories of composition
influenced by Japanese art – rather out of harmony
with the very traditional subject-matter.

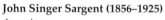

**John Singer Sargent (1856–1925)**
American
*On his holidays, Norway*, 1901–2
Oil on canvas; 137 x 244 cm
Purchased by Lever, 1923;
inv. no. LL 3136 (WHL 4730)

Alexander McCulloch, then a schoolboy at
Winchester College, is resting after salmon
fishing in Norway. The summer holidays
were a bad time for salmon fishing in
Britain and, with better communications,
Norway became more fashionable at the
end of the 19th century. Alexander was
the son of the great collector, George
McCulloch, from whose sale Lever bought
many of the late Victorian masterpieces in
the Main Hall. Sargent is best known for
his dazzling society portraits of the 1880s
and 1890s, and the descriptive power of
his rapid, vigorous brush strokes is very
evident here. After 1900 he gradually
abandoned formal portraiture in favour of
landscape, and the boy's casual but
thoughtful pose within a carefully worked
out natural setting very much reflects the
artist's new and rather wider intentions.

**John William Waterhouse (1849–1917)**
British
*The Decameron*, 1915–16
Oil on canvas; 101 x 159 cm
Purchased by Lever from the artist,
1916; inv. no. LL 3133 (WHL 2754)

Boccaccio's *Decameron* of about 1353 relates the often rather picturesque and risqué stories told to each other by a group of young men and women who had taken refuge in the countryside from the plague in Florence. Suppressed sexual tension and emotion in the contrasted faces and very varied attitudes of the women is given added poignancy by the idyllic garden setting. The lutes, too, signify love and the artist has achieved great dramatic intensity from his static and motionless composition.

**Alfred Jones Munnings (1878–1959)**
British
*The Friesian Bull*, 1920–21
Oil on canvas; 95.3 x 129 cm
Purchased from the artist by the
Trustees of the Lady Lever Art
Gallery, 1947; inv. no. LL 3915 (LP 69)

Munnings was both the most distinguished British animal painter of the 20th century and very interested in farming and country life. Naturally, therefore, he was fascinated by the new and immensely expensive black and white Friesian bulls which were changing the face of English dairy farming in the early 20th century. Here he contrasts the enormous bulk and power of the animal with its apparent placidity as it is led out by the herdsman. He actually witnessed the scene on the Devonshire farm of friends and found it pictorially irresistible. The free and rapid technique reflects his early style; his later work is more finished and detailed.

**Maurice Ferrary (1852–1904)**
French
*Salammbo*, 1899
Marble and bronze;
272 x 89 x 100.5 cm
Purchased by Lever from the
sculptor, 1900;
inv. no. LL 205 (TM 401)

Flaubert's great historical novel, *Salammbo*, of 1862 relates that, during the wars between the Carthaginians and the barbarians in the 3rd century B.C., Salammbo, the daughter of the Carthaginian leader, 'entwined herself with the genius of her family, with the very religion of her country under its most ancient symbol', that is with the huge snake. With this sacred protection she then went out to the barbarian camp to retrieve the famous veil, the loss of which had caused defeat for the Carthaginians. This subject, widely condemned as indecent even within Flaubert's novel, was very popular with a group of late 19th-century French sculptors preoccupied with erotic and sensual themes.

**William Goscombe John (1860–1952)**
British
*A Maid so Young (Childhood)*, 1896–7
Gilt bronze; 41 (with plinth) x 15 x 18 cm
Presented to the Gallery by Mrs Muriel Fildes, 1953;
inv. no. LL 701

The model for this bust was the sculptor's young daughter, who presented it to the Gallery many years later. Children in quiet, pensive moods had a special appeal to the artists of the 'New Sculpture', which, with its poetic realism, was the dominant force in British sculpture at the end of the 19th century. The strange bonnet adds a note of fantasy and imagination to the young face.

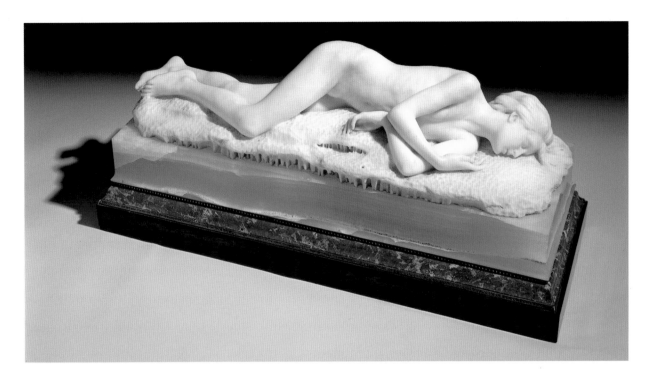

**Edward Onslow Ford (1852–1901)**
British
*Snowdrift*, 1901
Marble, green onyx, lapis lazuli with
silver mounts, black marble;
39.5 x 90.5 x 35.6 cm
Purchased by Lever from the artist's
executors, 1911; inv. no. LL 47 (H 540)

The figure is conceived as a personification of snow, or perhaps of the spirit of
winter, and here, with the coming of spring, the snow is melting and she is
sleeping – or dying. The sculptor combines intense poetry in the unusual pose
and haunting expression of the girl with direct realism in the modelling of her
figure: even her ribs are visible through her emaciated and bony flesh. His use
of varied materials and textures also reflects his adherence to the principles of
the 'New Sculpture'.

**Francis Derwent Wood (1872–1926)**
British
*The Penitent Thief*, 1918
Bronze; 35.5 x 28 x 23.5 cm
Presented to the Gallery by the sculptor's widow, 1945;
inv. no. LL 729 (LS 13)

The poetic realism for which the sculptors of the 'New
Sculpture' became famous in the last years of the 19th
century became weakened under a deluge of commissions
for rather conventional busts and monuments. Religious
subject matter, so rich in opportunities for expression and
meaning, was rare. This head, showing one of the two
thieves crucified alongside Christ, is therefore of particular
interest as it demonstrates so powerfully the sculptor's
ability to manipulate and model surfaces with deep
furrows and high, sharp ridges in order to produce a face
of enormous power and poignancy.

# chapter 2

# Furniture

The Gallery's holdings of furniture range in date from the late 16th century to the beginning of the 19th, embracing what in Lever's lifetime was considered to be the definitive period of fine English cabinet-making. Lever indeed was one of the earliest collectors to attempt to form a comprehensive collection of English furniture across this period, illustrating the salient features of successive styles; and the Lady Lever furniture collection constitutes one of his greatest achievements in the campaign to demonstrate the merits of British art. There is a certain irony in this, for Lever's intuitive liking for virtuosity and colour was much more naturally attuned to Continental taste, and led him to pursue the very grandest English furniture, which for much of the period in question was powerfully influenced by Continental, primarily French, styles. This is especially true of the outstanding group of marquetry and painted commodes (a type of low cabinet or chest of drawers – see pp. 53–8) of the 1760s to 1780s, by far Lever's favourite period within the long span covered by his collections.

In some cases, Lever's taste drew him to objects that time has shown actually to have originated on the Continent, such as the French 17th-century cabinet-on-stand (p. 44) – though this is of a type made all over Europe, Britain included – and the remarkable 18th-century beadwork urn, once thought to be English but now believed to have been made in Brunswick (p. 58). But in at least one context Lever deliberately acquired French furniture – when the objects in question were known or supposed to have had some connection with his political hero Napoleon. The original 'Napoleon Room' in the Lady Lever Art Gallery (Fig. 8), then twice the size of the space it now occupies, was filled with furniture and other objects that Lever had acquired for their associations with the Emperor, including the Fesch suite and Orchardson's sitter's chair (p. 65).

The Napoleon Room is one of five 'period rooms' in the Gallery, and distinct from the others in being not only devoted to a French style, but concerned with a personal cult. The other four are primarily intended to provide an appropriate setting for the furniture displayed in them: a decorative device that Lever also adopted in his houses, though then usually with new panelling made in the style of earlier periods. In the partly didactic context of the Lady Lever Art Gallery, he purchased genuine panelling for three of the rooms there, between 1917 and 1919. The 'Tudor & Stuart Room', from Lambourne Hall in Essex (Fig. 9), and the 'William & Mary Room', said to be from Walterclough Hall near Halifax, were both bought from Litchfield & Co., while the 'Early 18th-Century Room', from a house near Chatham, Kent, came from Arthur Edwards; but in all three cases the panelling had to be adapted and extended to fit the appointed spaces. The 'Adam Room', however, is an entirely new creation (apart from the 18th-century chimney-piece): it was designed for the Gallery by the furniture historian and stage designer Percy Macquoid, and executed by the firm of White Allom in 1924–5; the plasterwork is based on early Adam interiors of the 1760s, but arranged so densely as to make the room unmistakably Edwardian, and hence in some respects the most successful of all the period rooms.

Fig. 8 The Napoleon Room, *c*.1922. In the 1960s this space was divided into two rooms, one of which forms the present Napoleon Room.

While the period rooms provided a quasi-historical context for Lever's presentation of successive developments in English furniture, it is the furniture shown outside these rooms, almost all of it 18th-century, that reveals his main personal preferences. Next to the 'Adam' and other neo-classical furniture, perhaps the greatest strength of the collection is the peculiarly English Palladian-style furniture that evolved under the influence of William Kent in the 1720s–40s, of which Lever was a pioneer collector. At its most architectural, and Kentian, this style can be seen in the work of William Hallett – the mahogany cabinet from Kirtlington Park and the chairs from Longford Hall (pp. 48–9) – and in the anonymous gilt and painted side tables from Stowe (p. 47). Aspects of the style, such as the lion's masks and the shell motif, were also absorbed into the more domestic idiom of the period, as seen in the suite of walnut chairs by Thomas Moore (p. 46).

William Hallett was one of the most distinguished cabinet-makers of his generation, whose influence touched the careers of several younger men in the same trade. John Cobb, who in the 1770s gained a high reputation for his marquetry (see p. 55), was for some years in partnership with Hallett's former journeyman William Vile, and Vile & Cobb between them enjoyed a brief but highly productive period (1761–4) in service to the Royal Household. Hallett also promoted the career of his own nephew Samuel Norman – who may have made the mahogany commode on p. 53 – by introducing him to James Whittle as a suitable son-in-law and partner.

Fig. 9 The Tudor & Stuart Room, *c.*1922, with the state bed from Dyrham Park (where it has now been returned on loan). The overmantel on the left is inlaid with the initials and date, T.B. (supposedly for Thomas Barfoot), 1571, but these are now thought to be 19th-century additions; the panelling dates mainly from the early 17th century.

Another major London cabinet-making dynasty was that of William and John Linnell, father and son, initially established by William as a carving workshop in the 1720s, and carried on by John until two or three years before his death in 1796. One of their most celebrated joint commissions was the 'Chinese' bedroom suite at Badminton, supplied in the early 1750s, to which a pair of japanned china stands now in the Gallery belongs (p. 51). In the 1740s William had taken the imaginative step of sending his son to study at Hogarth's St. Martin's Lane Academy; and by the late 1760s John, now in charge of the firm, was working in a sophisticated marquetry idiom, the designs drawn with a fluency that owes much to this unusual training (p. 54). The style shows strong French influence, doubtless filtered through the Swedish cabinet-makers Georg Haupt and Christopher Fuhrlohg, whom Linnell employed briefly when they first arrived in London in 1767 or '68, having just completed their training in Paris. While Haupt was soon summoned back to Sweden to become the King's cabinet-maker, Fuhrlohg remained in London and set up in business on his own account, producing furniture that, while unmistakably English, is of very pronounced French character (see p. 54).

Thomas Chippendale, now the most famous name in the history of English furniture, lacked the dynastic advantages enjoyed by several of his rivals. Born and trained in Yorkshire, he arrived in London without connections in the late 1740s; and the publication in 1754 of *The Gentleman and Cabinet-maker's Director*, on which his posthumous reputation largely rests, was an astute attempt to compensate for these deficiences and make a very public bid for patronage. By 1762, when he published a third edition, he was in a position to boast that some of the designs had already been executed and had given 'entire satisfaction' (p. 52). But by this date he was already moving away from the rococo style that dominates the *Director*, towards the new classicism promoted by Robert Adam (p. 53).

The long-lived partnership of John Mayhew and William Ince (1758/9–1804), whose work is particularly well-represented in the Lady Lever collection (pp. 56–7), was also one of the most ambitious and innovative of their generation. Although only newly established in business, they responded directly to the publication of the *Director* with a rival work, published in 1762, *The Universal System of Household Furniture*. Like the *Director*, it featured designs almost entirely in the rococo style, and – like Chippendale – Mayhew & Ince were already experimenting with the 'antique' taste within a very few years of its appearance. On several commissions they worked closely with leading architects, especially Robert Adam in the 1760s–80s, and later Henry Holland.

A tradesman of a later generation who, like Chippendale, arrived in London from the provinces, was the so-called 'peintre-ébéniste' ('painter-cabinet-maker') George Brookshaw, unusual for focusing almost entirely on painted furniture (p. 61). He regularly advertised his specialist output in the London newspapers, and on at least one occasion attracted the custom of the Prince of Wales. But after twenty years' activity, he appears to have gone out of business in the mid-1790s, and temporarily assumed a false name (perhaps in order to conceal himself from creditors). When he resurfaced under his own name in 1804, it was as a teacher of flower-painting (a pursuit he had followed as a sideline while making furniture) and as the author and illustrator of an ambitious publication on fruit-growing, the *Pomona Britannica.*

Brookshaw's furniture was typically painted (and partly gilt) all over the surface, with no wood showing. But a slightly later fashion was for satinwood furniture with painted decoration on the wood, and the firm of Seddon, Sons & Shackleton is particularly known for this technique (see p. 62). Unlike Brookshaw, however, Seddons were an all-purpose firm operating on an enormous scale, and painted furniture was only one of their many branches of activity. Also unlike Brookshaw, the firm was exceptionally long-lived: founded by George Seddon in about 1753, it lasted, under various guises, until 1868.

Among the surprises yielded by recent furniture studies is the calibre of some furniture made outside London during the 18th century. The extraordinary suite of 'Chinese' rococo chairs (p. 51) is now known to have been made by a cabinet-maker operating in Berwick-upon-Tweed, by no means a major commercial centre. With hindsight, a provincial origin for this suite is entirely credible, for it is very much an aberration in terms of mainstream London furniture making – and it was doubtless its bizarre quality that largely appealed to Lever.

This suite also represents another significant strand in Lever's taste – his interest in the chinoiserie idiom in English furniture, ranging from the literal imitations of Oriental lacquer cabinets, favoured in the late 17th century (p. 45), to the more inventive creations of the rococo, such as the Badminton bedroom suite (see p. 51), the Chippendale dressing-table (p. 52) and above all these chairs. The exceptionally rare painted leather chairs from Parham Park (p. 45) reflect a half-way point between these two approaches; while the Anglo-Indian buffalo-horn chair (p. 60) is a late 18th-century manifestation of the same pursuit of the exotic; and the remarkable collector's cabinet (p. 64) is now thought to belong to an early 19th-century revival of the 'Chinese' rococo style. Such objects were completely in tune with Lever's taste for the strange and rare, a taste that he also gratified in many other areas of his collection. It is pieces of this nature, in some cases unique, in others simply the most outstanding examples of their kind, that make Lever's furniture collection not only highly personal, but also, judged by the most exacting and objective standards, one of the most distinguished collections ever to have been assembled.

**Nonsuch chest**
German or English, dated 1592; the stand
*c*.1900
Oak inlaid with rosewood, maple, box(?)
and green-stained holly or sycamore, with
wrought iron handles and hinges, on ash
stand; chest 56 x 122.5 x 57.5 cm (height
with stand 100 cm)
Presented to the Gallery by Mrs Percy
Macquoid, 1927; inv. no. LL 4723 (L 6)

Chests of this type acquired the name
'Nonsuch' from the mistaken belief that
they portray Henry VIII's famous palace in
Cheam. The buildings depicted are actually
in a conventional 'antique' style found on
16th-century furniture from southern
Germany, especially Cologne. However,
this chest could also have been made in
London by one of the German community
settled in Southwark (outside the
jurisdiction of the London guilds). Its
history is unknown before 1890 when the
furniture historian Percy Macquoid bought
it at the sale of William Maskell of Bude
Haven, Cornwall. The stand was made
later, apparently by Macquoid himself.
Theresa Macquoid presented the chest and
stand to commemorate her husband's
association with the Gallery, for which at
Lever's request he designed the Adam
Room and wrote the original catalogue of
the furniture collection.

**Cabinet-on-stand**
French, *c*.1680
Olive veneer with marquetry of ebony,
ivory, green-stained bone, box, sabicu and
other woods, ebonized beech(?) feet and
mouldings, gilt wood carving and brass
mounts, on a pine carcase, with walnut,
pine and oak drawers;
188.5 x 135 x 51 cm
Purchased by Lever, 1918;
inv. no. LL 4237 (X 266)

The cabinet was the most prestigious type
of furniture, apart from the state bed, in the
17th century (and gave rise to the English
term 'cabinet-maker' for the most skilled of
the wood-working trades). Similar
examples to this were made throughout
northern Europe, often with a matching
suite comprising a pier table, mirror and
candlestands. This piece appears to be
inspired by the outstanding, jewel-like
cabinets from the workshop of Pierre Gole,
cabinet-maker to the French Court. The
back of one of the small drawers is
inscribed 'Baudory', perhaps the name of a
previous owner.

**Cabinet-on-stand**
The cabinet Dutch(?), *c.*1690;
the stand English, *c.*1680
Japanned pine and oak with brass mounts, and
silvered pine stand;
cabinet 87.5 x 89 x 51.5 cm,
stand 79.5 x 114 x 57 cm,
overall height 165 cm
Cabinet purchased by Lever, 1918;
inv. no. LL 4474 (X 2648)
Stand of unknown provenance;
inv. no. LL 4475

The craze in the late 17th century for all things
oriental – porcelain, silks and lacquer especially –
created a demand that could not be met by the
imports of the Dutch and English East India
Companies, and the gap was filled by European
imitations, which were not necessarily considered
inferior. This cabinet in imitation lacquer, generally
known as japanning, is a direct translation of a
Japanese form, with its distinctive bracket base.
The silvered stand, inspired by Louis XIV's solid
silver furniture at Versailles, is roughly
contemporary but not the original one for this
cabinet.

**Chair**
English, *c.*1705–10
Beech and walnut, upholstered in gilt and painted
leather, close-nailed; 101.5 x 51.8 x 56.3 cm
Purchased by Lever, 1920;
inv. no. LL 4102 (X 4070)

One of a set of seven chairs from Parham Park,
Sussex, which retain their original upholstery and
gilt leather covers, an exceptionally rare survival.
The Chinese theme of the painted decoration is
also carried through to the seat frames: such
features as the 'ears' near the feet are inspired by
Chinese furniture of the sort made for the home
market, very little of which was exported to
Europe at this period. The shape of the back
resembles a celebrated set of needlework-covered
chairs at Canons Ashby, Northamptonshire,
supplied in 1714 by the Royal upholsterer Thomas
Phill. Phill also delivered an armchair (now lost)
covered in 'black Spanish Leather' with a nailed
border, which sounds comparable to the Parham
chairs.

**Settee**
English, c.1723; the tapestry c.1610
Walnut (veneered and solid) with
marquetry of holly and apple(?), oak
rails, wool and silk tapestry covers;
113.7 x 122.5 x 75.9 cm
Purchased by Lever, 1920;
inv. no. LL 4234 (X 3846)

The arms painted on the cresting are those of Thomas Wyndham of Hawkchurch, Dorset, and Elizabeth Helyar of Yately, Hampshire, who were married in about 1723. The settee, doubtless made to commemorate the marriage, is possibly of provincial manufacture; the initials C.P., perhaps those of the maker, are branded on the oak seat frame. The curiously high back and deep seat suggest the settee was specially made to frame the Sheldon tapestry cushion covers, depicting the virtues of Faith, Charity, Hope, Justice and Temperance, which were then over a hundred years old: an unusual antiquarian gesture at that period.

**Chair**
**Thomas Moore (d. 1738)**
English, 1734
Walnut, beech and oak, later cover of voided
cotton-velvet; 98.6 x 63.5 x 62 cm
Acquired by Lever, 1903 or 1904;
inv. no. LL 4127 (H 495)

One of a suite of eight (but originally ten) chairs supplied to Sir Dudley Ryder in 1734 by Thomas Moore, formerly the partner of Daniel Bell (the partnership appears to have been dissolved in the same year, when Bell was appointed cabinet-maker and chair-maker to the Royal Household). The chairs were described on Moore's bill as 'ten hansome Wallnuttree Chairs broad banister backs cutt in a shape with scrole tops finneard [veneered] with very good wood, loose compass seats ... with rich carved fore feet with Lyons faces on Ye Knees and Lyons Paws & O. Ge [ogee] back feet with scroles and carved shells to ye fore rails'. The bill also records another similar suite of walnut chairs and a pair of gilt wood pier tables and mirrors *en suite*. No charge is noted for travelling expenses, so this furniture may have been delivered to a London house.

## Side-table

English, *c*.1740
Gilt and painted pine, the top
veneered in calcite 'onyx', with
solid white marble borders;
88 x 189.5 x 97 cm
Purchased by Lever, 1919;
inv. no. LL 4232 (X 3743)

Decorated with masks of Diana
(a crescent moon in her hair)
and satyrs, this table and its
pair were at Stowe House,
Buckinghamshire, until the
great sale of 1848 when they
were bought by Sir Philip
Pauncefort-Duncombe for
Great Brickhill Manor nearby.
A generation earlier than the
Stowe state bed (see p. 50),
they are in the Palladian style
associated with William Kent,
who indeed was employed at
Stowe by Lord Cobham in the
1730s. The tops are probably
early 19th-century
replacements, that is, 18th-
century veneered slabs,
extended by new borders fixed
with big brass studs.

## Armchair

Scottish(?), *c*.1740
Gilt pine and beech, covers of
linen canvas embroidered in
wool and silk in tent-stitch;
108 x 81.3 x 67.4 cm
Purchased by Lever, 1918;
inv. no. LL 4205 (X 2973)

The embroidery on the back
depicts the *Sacrifice of Iphigenia*,
the post-Homeric story that
Agamemnon's daughter was
sacrificed to appease the
goddess Artemis, who had
induced a calm to prevent the
Greek fleet sailing to Troy; here
Agamemnon and Achilles look
on as, at the last minute,
Artemis takes pity and spirits
Iphigenia away. The seat is
embroidered more simply with
a dog chasing a fox. These
covers are original and the
borders show that they were
specially designed for this
chair. It is one of an original set
of at least six, and several other
examples with very similar
embroidery are known, mostly
from houses in Scotland.

**Settee**
English, *c.*1760
Gilt beech, covers of linen canvas embroidered in wool and
silk in tent stitch and cross-stitch, decorative brass nails,
and red moreen on the back; 102.5 x 223.2 x 88.4 cm
Purchased by Lever, 1919; inv. no. LL 4226 (X 3350)

The covers, which may be original, depict pastoral scenes
and vases of flowers in cartouches. The scene at the left end
of the back is adapted from an engraving, *Le Soir*, one of the
series *Les Pastorales*, engraved by Claudine Stella after
designs by her uncle Jacques Stella, and published in Paris
in 1664. Such subjects strongly appealed to rococo taste a
century later.

**Chair**
**Attributed to William Hallett (*c.*1707–1781)**
English, *c.*1737–40
Virginia walnut, solid and veneered, and
partly gilt; beech seat rails; original drop-in
caned seat beneath the later fixed
upholstery and wool-velvet cover;
96 x 59.6 x 62 cm
Purchased by Lever, 1917;
inv. no. LL 4064 (X 2020)

One of a set of five chairs which almost
certainly originated at Holkham Hall,
Norfolk, seat of the Cokes, Earls of
Leicester; but they were sold from another
Coke family house, Longford Hall,
Derbyshire, in 1917. The model is inspired
by the designs of William Kent, the architect
of Holkham and creator of the Palladian
style in interior decoration. Two variant
chairs remain at Holkham –  the finer one
probably a 'pattern chair' (see p. 51) that
William Hallett made for Lord Leicester's
approval in 1738. The other was probably
ordered locally, in an attempt to procure the
set more cheaply – but the final commission
was evidently given to Hallett after all.
The chairs have drop-in caned seats beneath
the later upholstery, an unusual feature also
found in another set of Kentian chairs at
Holkham.

**Cabinet-on-chest**
**Attributed to William Hallett (*c*.1707–1781)**
English, *c*.1747
Sabicu(?) and purplewood veneer with brass inlay and
mounts and mahogany carvings, partly gilt, on a carcase of
mahogany (the upper section) and pine (lower section),
with drawers of mahogany (upper section) and oak (lower
section); 249 x 150 x 54 cm
Purchased by Lever, 1911;
inv. no. LL 4416 (HH 188)

This stylish Palladian cabinet comes from Kirtlington Park,
Oxfordshire, which was built about 1742–6 by Sir James
Dashwood. It was probably made by William Hallett, the
principal cabinet-maker employed by Sir James in
furnishing the house, who was paid £425 in 1747 and
further smaller sums up to 1752. The striking male terms
supporting the base section suggest that it was intended for
a room with a very specific, and imposing, decorative
programme. The carcase has latterly been raised by about
two inches between these figures.                              **49**

**State bed**
**Designed by Giovanni Battista Borra (1712–1786)**
English, 1757–9
Gilt mahogany and pine (the gilding renewed), silk taffeta, gilt and red rope; embroidery of gold, red and blue metal foil, gold and silver metal thread, silver and steel spangles, silk on card or vellum, coloured paste jewels and beads, with silk-velvet, pearls and metal thread fringe; modern red silk shantung and yellow watered silk hangings with wool and silk galloon and fringe;
447.5 x 297.5 x 272 cm approx.
Purchased by Lever at the Stowe House sale, 1921; inv. no. LL 4207 (X 4091)

Designed by the Piedmontese architect G.B. Borra, for the State Bedroom at Stowe House, Buckinghamshire. Borra had accompanied Robert Wood and James Dawkins on their celebrated expedition to Baalbec and Palmyra in 1750–51, a seminal event in the creation of English neo-classicism. This bed is a rococo creation, however, reflecting Borra's training in his native Turin. It was originally hung with Genoese crimson damask. The coat of arms and cypher, in the headboard and canopy respectively, are late 18th-century work but were introduced to the bed when it was refurbished for Queen Victoria's visit to Stowe in 1845. The remaining hangings reflect the scheme adopted at that time, but all except the crimson silk in the canopy are modern replacements.

## Chairs
**William Davidson (c.1729–1773)**
English (Berwick-upon-Tweed), c.1766
Mahogany, beech and pine, modern silk
damask covers; 105.8 x 67.9 x 72.3 cm,
105.3 x 67.2 x 70 cm
Purchased by Lever, 1915;
inv. nos. LL 4068 (X 419),
LL 4072 (X 416)

Two remarkable chinoiserie chairs from a set of seven (and a much altered sofa),
made for Sir John (later Lord) Delaval at Ford Castle, Northumberland. William
Davidson was evidently referring to this suite when he wrote from Berwick to Lady
Delaval at Ford, in 1766: 'your 6 Chenise Chairs & fly table shall be sett about and
forwarded in dew time. To your desire have sent you a Pattron Chair ... it is
wanting 2 Brass Buttons behind'. The chair on the left is the pattern chair, with
different options for the treatment of the seat rails: the other chair shows further
modifications that were adopted for the rest of the suite. The loose backs are indeed
held in place by two swivelling brass 'buttons' in the form of Chinamen's masks.

## China stand
**William Linnell (c.1703–1763) and John Linnell (1729–1796)**
English, 1752–4
Japanned pine and mahogany; 149 x 50.6 x 26 cm
Purchased by Lever, 1922; inv. no. LL 45 (X 4150)

One of a pair, which come from a celebrated suite of furniture made by
the Linnells for the 'Chinese' state bedchamber at Badminton House,
Gloucestershire. The state bed is now in the Victoria & Albert Museum,
together with the commode and two of the eight armchairs. A drawing by
John Linnell (William's son) for the chairs suggests that he probably
designed the entire suite, although the workshop was still run by his
father at this date. The drawing shows a different colour scheme in red,
blue and yellow, traces of which have been found on some of the other
pieces in the suite: the present scheme probably dates from the mid- or
late 19th century.

**Dressing-table**
**Thomas Chippendale**
**(1718–1779)**
English, c.1760
Rosewood (veneered and
solid) and simulated
rosewood graining, carved
oil-gilt mahogany and
water-gilt lime(?), brass
and ormolu mounts and
ivory handles, on a pine,
walnut, mahogany, oak
and lime(?) carcase;
206.2 x 128.5 x 62.5 cm
Purchased by Lever, 1916;
inv. no. LL 4245 (X 1608)

A 'Chinese' variation on a
rococo design published by
Chippendale in the 3rd
edition (1762) of *The
Gentleman and Cabinet-
Maker's Director* (plate LII),
and probably one of those
that he referred to in
commenting on this plate:
'Two Dressing-Tables have
been made of Rose-Wood,
from this Design, which
gave an entire Satisfaction:
All the Ornaments were
gilt.' It was probably made
for Lady Arniston, who
was a client of
Chippendale's and whose
descendants sold it in 1916.
Notable features of this
piece include the hinged
brass brackets on which the
mirror moves backwards
and forwards, and the
carved wood – not metal –
open fretwork of the upper
cupboard doors.

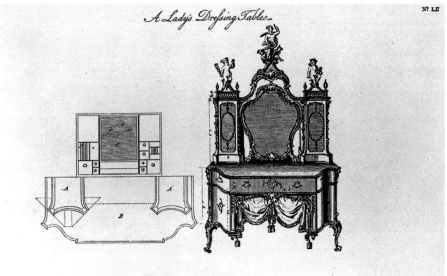

Fig. 10 Thomas
Chippendale, *The
Gentleman and Cabinet-
maker's Director*, 3rd edition
(1762), plate 52, 'A Lady's
Dressing Table'

**Commode**
**Thomas Chippendale (1718–1779)**
English, *c.*1775–80
Marquetry of East Indian satinwood, tulipwood, purplewood, fruitwoods, rosewood, sycamore, harewood and box, with ormolu and lacquered brass mounts, on a pine and rosewood carcase, with mahogany and oak drawers; 91 x 147.5 x 62.5 cm
Purchased by Lever, 1914; inv. no. LL 4247 (X 19)

This commode has strong stylistic affinities with the neo-classical furniture supplied by Thomas Chippendale to Harewood House in the 1770s, such as put his authorship of this piece beyond doubt. But it is not known for whom, or for what house, it was originally made. It was allegedly given away by the Duke of Wellington to his campaign chaplain, probably in the 1820s or '30s; and the pair to it, now in a private collection, appears to have been acquired at about the same time by a Liverpool merchant and politician, Ashton Yates.

**Commode**
English, *c.*1765
Mahogany veneer and carving with gilt metal mounts, on a pine, oak and mahogany carcase; 87.5 x 129 x 60 cm
Purchased by Lever, 1913;
inv. no. LL 48 (H 45)

In this rococo masterpiece the serpentine form is complemented by outstanding carving of scrolls, shells and foliage, and by the asymmetric gilt metal mounts, chased with similar motifs. The commode came from the Western family of Felix Hall (and previously of Rivenhall) in Essex, but the existence of an identical example at Aske Hall, Yorkshire, suggests that both commodes were made by one of the London cabinet-makers patronized by Sir Lawrence Dundas at Aske and other houses in the 1760s – among them Samuel Norman, Francis Gilding, James Lawson and Lawrence Fell.

**Commode**
**John Linnell (1729–1796)**
English, *c.*1768–70
Marquetry of maple, purplewood,
rosewood, walnut, mahogany, holly,
fruitwoods, sycamore and other woods,
with ormolu mounts, on a pine,
mahogany and oak carcase;
86 x 107 x 46 cm
Purchased by Lever, 1919;
inv. no. LL 49 (X 3110)

This is related to furniture supplied by
John Linnell to Osterley Park,
Middlesex, in the late 1760s, as well as
to some designs for commodes among a
large group of Linnell's drawings (now
in the Victoria & Albert Museum),
which show him to have been an
accomplished draughtsman, as is
reflected in the drawing of the
marquetry cartouches and trophies on
this piece. This decoration perhaps also
reveals the influence of the Paris-
trained Swedish cabinet-makers, Georg
Haupt and Christopher Fuhrlohg, who
were briefly employed in his workshop
at about this time. The subjects of the
trophies, Music and Painting, suggest
the commode was intended for a
drawing room, devoted to the arts.

**Commode**
**Christopher Fuhrlohg (active
1762–1787)**
English, *c.*1772
Marquetry of harewood, tulipwood,
purplewood, sycamore, fruitwoods,
holly, walnut, mahogany, box, ebony
and other woods, with ormolu and
brass mounts, on an oak carcase with
mahogany drawers;
99.5 x 142.5 x 45.5 cm
Acquired by Lever, 1903 or 1904;
inv. no. LL 4233 (H 286)

The breakfront form and the trellis
parquetry reflect Fuhrlohg's recent
training in Paris (see p. 42), but the
medallion of Diana is in the distinctive
style of Angelica Kauffman, who
worked in London in the 1760s–70s.
Indeed the medallion on a companion
commode is signed in Latin,
'C. Fuhrlohg, 1772, after Angelica
Kauffman'. Fuhrlohg could have been
following original drawings by
Kauffman, for no engraved source for
either composition is known.
The doors have been converted from
sliding panels which originally ran on
tracks under the case. The marquetry in
the frieze is also a later introduction.

**Commode**
English, *c*.1770
Gilt and painted mahogany and pine, with ormolu and lacquered brass mounts;
88.5 x 143.5 x 72.5 cm
Acquired by Lever, 1903 or 1904; inv. no. LL 4376 (H 150)

This commode, from Seaton Delaval Hall, Northumberland, was originally fitted inside with '13 Copper front[ed] Drawers inlaid in mother of Pearl', and had a pair of corner cupboards *en suite*. The suite was sold to Sir John Delaval in 1776 by John Cobb, on commission from its owner John Carrack, a haberdasher and hosier, who seems to have been speculating in furniture (this suite had by then been on his hands for several years). The maker remains unidentified, but the *bombé* shape (curved in two planes at once), the construction and the decorative treatment all indicate an immigrant craftsman.

**Commode**
**John Cobb (*c*.1715–1778)**
English, *c*.1770
Marquetry of mahogany, satinwood, rosewood, tulipwood, sycamore, walnut, box, holly, purplewood, fruitwoods and birch, with lacquered brass mounts, on a mahogany and pine carcase;
92.5 x 115 x 60 cm
Purchased by Lever, 1920; inv. no. LL 56 (X 3733)

The top shows the coat of arms (with a baron's coronet) of the commode's first owner Lord Hyde, later created Earl of Clarendon. Cobb's most celebrated work is a slightly larger marquetry commode of very similar design and construction to this one, which he supplied to Paul Methuen at Corsham Court, Wiltshire in 1772, with a pair of candlestands *en suite*.

55

**Commode**
**John Mayhew (1736–1811)**
**& William Ince (d. 1804)**
English, *c.*1773
Marquetry of birch, satinwood, tulipwood, kingwood, holly, avodire(?), fruitwoods, purplewood, walnut, ebony, box and sycamore, with ormolu and lacquered brass mounts, on a mahogany and pine carcase; 90.5 x 132 x 64.5 cm
Purchased by Lever at the Earl of Home's sale, 1919; inv. no. LL 57 (X 3398)

This handsome commode was supplied to Archibald Douglas (later created Lord Douglas) for his London house in Pall Mall, which he was also filling with French furniture in the early 1770s (much of it smuggled in under diplomatic cover). Following French practice, the commode came with a pair of corner cupboards *en suite* (which are now in an American collection). The simple box-like form, contrasting with the very elaborate decoration, was pioneered by Mayhew & Ince in the 1760s; it must have seemed startlingly austere at a time when English commodes were, almost by definition, serpentine.

**Commode**
**John Mayhew (1736–1811) &**
**William Ince (d. 1804)**
English, *c.*1780
Marquetry of makore(?), kingwood, tulipwood, purplewood, sycamore, box, ivory, ebony, holly, fruitwoods and other woods, with ormolu mounts, on a mahogany and pine carcase; 84.5 x 144.5 x 61 cm
Acquired by Lever between 1901 and 1903;
inv. no. LL 4246 (H 526)

In this remarkable design, the bold serpentine shape of the top is echoed by the profile of the aprons in the opposite plane. The charging bull, derived from an antique gem, suggests this was part of a major iconographic scheme, and the apparently unique ormolu mounts also point to the high status of this still unidentified commission. A related (but less sophisticated) pair of commodes at Broadlands, Hampshire, were probably among the furniture supplied by Mayhew & Ince to Viscount Palmerston.

**Commode**

**John Mayhew (1736–1811) & William Ince (d. 1804)**

English, *c*.1775–80

Marquetry of harewood, ebony, holly, East Indian and West Indian satinwood, purplewood, hornbeam(?), rosewood, tulipwood, box and mahogany, with painted copper medallion and ormolu and lacquered brass mounts, on a mahogany and pine carcase; 90.5 x 138 x 56 cm

Purchased by Lever at the Bretby Heirlooms sale, 1918; inv. no. LL 4225 (X 2661)

In 1774 Robert Adam designed the first so-called 'Etruscan' interior: the Countess of Derby's dressing-room at Derby House in London, inspired by the decoration of Greek vases (which then were thought to be Etruscan – see p. 94): the commode for the room was manufactured by Mayhew & Ince, who subsequently adapted the model (with or without Adam's consent) for other clients. This version, centring a painted copper medallion of Cupid and the Three Graces, belonged to the Earls of Chesterfield, and was probably ordered by the 5th Earl for Chesterfield House in Mayfair.

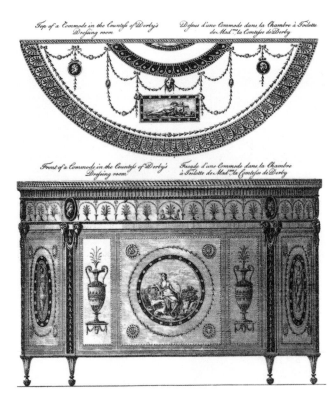

Fig. 11 Robert Adam's design for the Derby House commode, engraved in 1777 for *The Works in Architecture of Robert and James Adam* (1778–9), Vol. II, Part I, plate 8

**Commode**
English, *c*.1765–70
Oak, partly gilt, the top
veneered in red breccia marble;
91.5 x 141.5 x 72 cm
Purchased by Lever, 1918;
inv. no. LL 4321 (X 2922)

The use of solid oak as a show
wood on an object of such
grandeur is seemingly
unparalleled in English 18th-
century furniture. It was
presumably used at the request
of the patron, and may have
come from a tree with
particular associations. The
carved and gilt angles and feet
are copied from contemporary
gilt metal mounts. This
commode may be from the
same (unidentified) workshop
as a group of lacquer and
japanned commodes that
feature these mounts, but one
of which has the same patterns
in gilt wood, as here.

**Urn-on-stand**
German (Brunswick), *c*.1760
Glass beads, enamel plaques, shells,
mother-of-pearl, agate, wool embroidery
and gilt metal mounts, on a pine core,
with later gilt wood finial;
170.5 x 50 x 49.2 cm
Purchased by Lever, 1919;
inv. no. LL 4267 (X 3686–7)

This was probably made in the specialist workshop
established in Brunswick by an apparently Dutch
immigrant, Johann Michael van Selow, active from 1755 to
1767; however, most of the production was flat panels for
table-tops and few three-dimensional pieces like this are
known. Stylistically this is still a baroque object, an
indication of the provincial character of North German
taste at a time when, elsewhere in Europe, the rococo was
at its height. The only trace of the rococo to be found here is
in the coarse gilt metal mounts under the 'cover' of the urn
and at the base.

## Globe clock
**Jean Romilly (1714–1796)**
French, c.1765–70
Bronze, ormolu and enamel; 113.3 x 71.5 x 63.6 cm
Purchased by Lever at the Stafford House sale, 1913;
inv. no. LL 4464 (HH 241)

The time is marked by the central band revolving past the
serpent's tongue. Three putti share the burden of the Earth,
traditionally borne by Atlas. Their attributes represent the
four elements: Earth (the rock they stand on), Fire (coming
out of the rock), Water (spilling from the ewer) and Air (in
their billowing draperies).
The clock may have been designed by the leading
*marchand-mercier* (a sort of dealer-cum-decorator) Simon-
Philippe Poirier, for whom Romilly sometimes worked. Its
early history is unknown, but by 1839 it was at Stafford
House, the opulent town house of the Duke of Sutherland:
it stood on its present pedestal in the ground-floor Drawing
Room, in the centre of a circular ottoman upholstered in
'Purple & Amber Satin, with a deep silk fringe'.
Lever bought a number of works of art at the Stafford
House sale in 1913; he also purchased the house itself,
which he renamed Lancaster House and presented to the
nation to become the first home of the Museum of London.

## Dressing-table
French, c.1770–90
Straw marquetry on a poplar(?) carcase;
74.6 x 91.5 x 45.5 cm
Purchased by Lever, 1910;
inv. no. LL 4619 (H 218)

As with the filigree paper cabinet
(p. 60), this is an unusually large
example of such a delicate material to
survive intact: it is the most ambitious
instance of the straw-work technique in
the Gallery's collection of some
hundred pieces. The pastoral scenes are
doubtless derived from engravings, like
the embroidered scenes on the rococo
settee (p. 48). The table is said to have
belonged to one of George III's
equerries, who could have acquired it
in Paris.

59

**Elbow chair**
Anglo-Indian, *c.*1780–90
Buffalo horn with gilt decoration, caned seat under later upholstery and figured satin cover, later painted and gilt iron(?) repair-straps; 90.4 x 57.1 x 54.3 cm
Purchased by Lever, 1919; inv. no. LL 4509 (X 3425)

This is similar in form to Anglo-Indian chairs made of ivory, but appears to be a unique surviving example in buffalo horn. It is said to have belonged to Warren Hastings, Governor General of India from 1774 to 1784, and almost certainly formed part of a present from an Indian princess to his wife in 1784. Hastings informed his wife that the gift included two chairs of 'buffalo horn most delicately formed, ... not designed for fat folks, nor romps; nor proper for you, my elegant Marion, to use in the presence of your husband'.

**Cabinet-on-stand**
English, *c.*1780–90
Filigree paper, mezzotints and beads, stained holly or sycamore and ebonized pear, and brass handles, on a pine carcase; 146.5 x 61.5 x 45 cm
Purchased by Lever, 1919; inv. no. LL 4224 (X 3733)

Filigree paperwork was a fashionable ladies' accomplishment in the 18th and early 19th centuries. In 1786 *The New Ladies' Magazine* published patterns 'suitable for tea-caddies, toilets, chimney-pieces, screens, cabinets, frames, picture ornament etc.'. Few pieces of full-scale furniture in this fragile medium now survive. This cabinet was sold by the descendants of the merchant John Julius Angerstein (1735–1823), whose picture collection forms the nucleus of the National Gallery. It could have been decorated by either of his two wives, or it may be a professional production.

**Secretaire commode**
**George Brookshaw (1751–1823)**
English, *c*.1785–90
Painted mahogany and pine,
gilt mahogany and composition
mouldings;
97 x 187.5 x 62.5 cm
Purchased by Lever, 1914;
inv. no. LL 4322 (X 20)

Originally from Birmingham,
George Brookshaw set up a
cabinet-making business in
London in 1777. His workshop
dealt almost exclusively in
painted furniture, typically with
closely observed floral
decoration and figurative
medallions adapted from
engravings, chiefly after
Angelica Kauffman. The
medallions on the present
commode (all derived from
Kauffman) represent *Una and
the Lion* (on top), and the lovers
*Damon and Musidora* and *Paris
and Oenone*. Brookshaw also
operated as a teacher of flower-
painting, and in the 1790s he
abandoned his furniture
practice in favour of publishing
drawing-manuals, and a
lavishly illustrated work on
fruit-growing, the *Pomona
Britannica*.

**Settee**
**Attributed to George
Brookshaw (1751–1823)**
English, *c*.1785
Gilt and painted beech(?), covers
decorated with knotting in silk,
re-applied to new silk ground;
100.6 x 215 x 79.7 cm
Acquired by Lever before 1907;
inv. no. LL 4160 (H 259)

Part of a suite of two settees and
six elbow chairs, formerly at
Berechurch Hall, Essex, painted
with scenes from literature and
mythology and with delicate
floral decoration in Brookshaw's
characteristic style. The frames
are now gilded all over, but
originally the ribbons around the
oval backs were picked out in
blue. The embroidered
seat-covers have been cut down
from larger pieces (perhaps
curtains); they were probably
put on this suite in the early
19th century.

**Writing-cabinet**
**Attributed to Seddon, Sons & Shackleton**
English, c.1795–1800
Satinwood, purplewood, satin birch and other
veneers, partly painted, on a mahogany carcase;
164.8 x 98.2 x 42 cm
Purchased by Lever, 1915;
inv. no. LL 4154 (X 294)

The design of this cabinet is highly sophisticated in its three-
dimensional play on sections of circles and ellipses. It is closely
comparable to a mahogany writing-table in the Metropolitan Museum,
New York, bearing the trade label of Seddon, Sons & Shackleton.
Thomas Sheraton also shows a related, but less complex, design in *The
Cabinet-Maker and Upholsterer's Drawing-Book* (1793), for a cabinet 'to
accommodate a lady with conveniences for writing, reading, and
holding her trinkets'. By 1901 this piece was in the collection of the
Liverpool shipper William Imrie, who also owned Burne-Jones's *The
Tree of Forgiveness*, now in the Gallery's collection.

## China-stand

English, *c.*1820
Gilt pine; 43 x 64 x 60 cm
Purchased by Lever, 1923;
inv. no. LL 4720 (X 4493/4)

One of a set of three stands, one for
three vases and two for a single
vase each, from Stowe House,
Buckinghamshire. They are carved
in the extravagant rococo-revival
style of the early 19th century, with
marine motifs: a central mask of
Neptune, surrounded by dolphins,
crabs, lobsters, turtles, frogs, a
variety of shells and rocks. The
cypher of entwined Bs with a
marquess's coronet shows that they
were made for the 2nd Marquess of
Buckingham before 1822, when he
was created Duke of Buckingham.
Lever may have bought the stands
to go with the mid-18th-century
state bed from Stowe (see p. 50), for
until recently they were believed to
date from the same period.

(Photographed in course of conservation)

## Writing-table
## Painted by John Thomas Serres (1759–1825)

English, *c.*1785–90, repainted 1792
Painted mahogany and pine with brass
mounts; 103.5 x 74 x 52.7 cm
Purchased by Lever, 1912;
inv. no. LL 46 (H 437)

The seascapes, mostly of British ports, are
signed and dated (1792) by J.T. Serres, Marine
Painter to George III, who must have been
commissioned to redecorate this writing-table
within a very few years of its initial
manufacture. To make his task easier, the table
was sawn up into flat components that could
be held on an easel, which were afterwards
nailed together again, and this crude
construction was disguised by the thick black
borders. Like these borders, the trophies at the
top of the legs are by a different hand; and
below these the legs retain their original (pre-
Serres) decoration. The table is in the form of a
French *bonheur-du-jour*, with a fitted
compartment on top, but its cupboard-doors
were nailed shut when the table was re-
assembled.

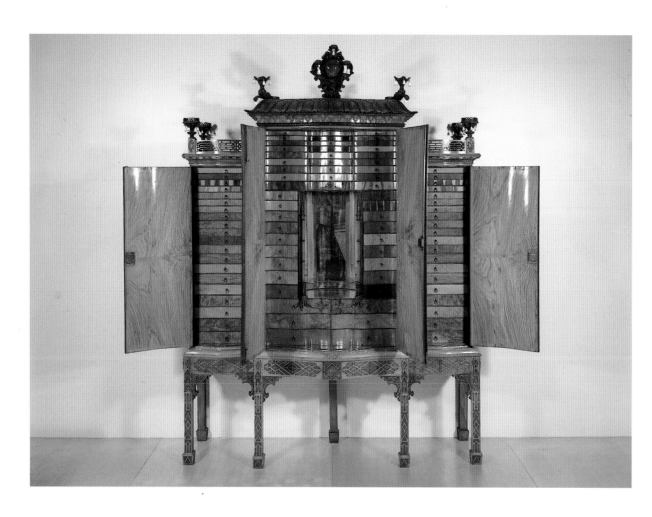

**Cabinet-on-stand**

English, *c.*1820–1830

Veneers of amboyna, padouk, pollard oak, walnut
and numerous other exotic and native woods,
rosewood and mahogany mouldings and ivory bells,
on an oak and mahogany carcase; the stand rosewood
and pine; 260.5 x 192.7 x 64 cm

Purchased by Lever from the Percy Dean sale, 1909;
presented to the Gallery by the 3rd Viscount
Leverhulme, 1980; inv. no. LL 4032 (H 159)

Though inspired by mid-18th-century models, such as
Chippendale's designs for 'China Cases' in *The
Gentleman and Cabinet-maker's Director*, this is now
thought to belong to the early 19th-century rococo
revival. It is a collector's cabinet, ultimately derived
from 17th-century examples (see pp. 44–5), and
probably intended for specimens of natural history –
the different woods veneered on the drawers also
forming a collection in themselves. It is said to have
come from the family of the Earls of Guilford, and
could possibly have been made for the Rev. Charles
Augustus North (1785–1825), grandson of the 1st Earl,
whose collection of porcelain, bronzes and French
furniture, as well as his 'valuable hot-house and
green-house plants', were sold after his death in 1825.

**Armchair**
**Designed by Dionisio Santi (b. 1786) and
Lorenzo Santi (1783–1839)**
Italian (Rome), c.1805–06
Gilt walnut and beech, silk embroidered covers
with silk-covered gimp; 106.4 x 75.7 x 73 cm
Purchased by Lever, 1919;
inv. no. LL 4640 (X 3621)

Typically Italian in its sculptural quality, this
belongs to a large suite designed by the Santi
brothers and made in Rome for Napoleon's
uncle Cardinal Fesch, who served as the
Emperor's ambassador to the Pope from 1803.
In 1806 Napoleon suddenly recalled him,
before the suite could be finished; and
following the battle of Waterloo it was sold –
still with no covers – from the Cardinal's house
in Paris in 1816. The embroidered covers
shown here were placed on the suite for the
collector George Watson Taylor, around 1820.
The chairs are now displayed with new silk
covers to protect the originals underneath.

**Armchair**
**Attributed to Jean-Jacques Werner (1791–1849)**
French, c.1815–20
Gilt beech (the gilding renewed), later silk
brocatelle covers; 109.1 x 68.6 x 66.1 cm
Purchased by Lever, 1913;
inv. no. LL 4286 (HH 249)

Like the Fesch furniture, Lever bought this
chair for its association with Napoleon, for it
was alleged to have been at his palace of
Malmaison until removed by the 1st Earl
Cowley, who was British ambassador to Paris
from 1852 to 1867. However, the chair is now
thought to date from after the fall of Napoleon;
and if it was indeed taken from Malmaison by
Lord Cowley, it cannot have been part of the
furnishings from Napoleon I's time, which
were sold in 1829. The crown in the centre of
the cresting is a later insertion.

# chapter 3

# Textiles

The Lady Lever Art Gallery's textiles collection is especially rich in examples of British embroidery, and in particular embroidered pictures of which it has over a hundred – one of the largest collections in the country. It also has fine items of 17th- and 18th-century costume, accessories and furnishings, including several tapestries from important series. But only half (approximately) of the embroidered pictures in Lever's possession at his death are now in the Gallery, the rest having been sold by his executors in 1925–6. (Another part of the collection, which decorated his Rivington bungalow, Roynton Cottage, was destroyed in 1913 in an arson attack by a suffragette.) The emphasis on embroidered pictures reflects collecting fashion at the beginning of the 20th century when Lever began buying embroideries. His interest was probably spurred by his furnishing of Hall-i'-th'-Wood, a house near his native town of Bolton, as a museum of 16th- and 17th-century domestic life. Almost all of this type of embroidery was worked by amateur young women and teenagers, either as part of their domestic education or to decorate their homes and fill their leisure hours. Lever was probably attracted to it partly because he saw it as proof of the high degree of decorative skill and technical craft that 'ordinary' British people could achieve.

The earliest examples of embroidery in the collection are a set of late 16th- or early 17th-century valances for a four-poster bed, embroidered with scenes illustrating the Old Testament story of Queen Athaliah and the boy king Joash (2 Kings verse 11 and 2 Chronicles verses 22–23). These had been turned into 'pictures' by framing and as such are typical of several 'pictures' in the collection, which were originally worked as furnishings to cover mirror frames, chair-backs, cushions and young women's work-caskets. Caskets were the culmination of a girl's domestic education and were often embroidered with Old Testament scenes considered most suitable by parent or governess for a teenage girl: the love match between Isaac and Rebecca or the intended sacrifice by Abraham of his son Isaac, one of the most commonly embroidered biblical scenes in 17th-century Britain, which could illustrate the Commandment of honouring your parents (see p. 70).

The Gallery has some fine examples of 17th-century mirror frames and caskets, several of which show the distinctive style of raised work, popular in the second half of the 17th century, in which padded figures in very high relief, as well as gold and silver thread and lace, mica and seed pearls, were incorporated into embroidered pictures. The collecting of raised work was popularized from the beginning of the 20th century by art publications, which often referred to it as 'stumpwork'. A prime example of the style is *The Drowning of the Pharaoh in the Red Sea* (p. 70). This picture is rare in having accompanying documentation which helped identify the embroideress and provided illuminating information about her social, economic and religious context. The collection also includes several other elaborately worked pictures from the Stuart period. Unlike these pieces, created by young amateurs, many of the 17th-century costume accessories, particularly the elaborate gloves never intended for daily wear (p. 71), were worked by professionals in workshops.

Fig. 12 The Gobelins tapestries hanging in the Dining Room at Lews Castle, *c.*1910

Not surprisingly, Lever was also attracted to 18th-century needlework which complemented his furniture collection. He acquired a number of pastoral scenes, most of which, as was common in the 18th century, were embroidered on fine linen canvas and intended either as furnishing textiles to cover screens, settees and chairs, or as pictures to decorate dressing-room walls and chimneypieces. More unusual among collectors of embroidered pictures was Lever's taste for late Georgian and Regency needleworks, which were partly embroidered, partly painted in watercolour onto silk (p. 71). Usually hands and faces, the most difficult details to embroider satisfactorily, were painted, and the rest of the picture embroidered – providing a way by which ladies could display their accomplishments in what was considered an especially feminine art form. The speckled stitches frequently used on these painted silk pictures recreated the effect of the stipple engravings, sometimes of works by women artists such as Angelica Kauffmann (1741–1806), that often provided the basis for designs. A growing number of these pictures have been identified as being based on theatrical and literary scenes.

Most of the small collection of tapestries was acquired between 1915 and 1920 and includes a number of important works. The Gobelins group came from Lews Castle, Stornoway, and Lever purchased them in 1918, at the same time as buying the castle itself with the Isle of Lewis (Fig. 12). Lews Castle had been built in 1847 and lavishly furnished in a 'baronial' style by another Victorian entrepreneur businessman, Sir James Matheson (d. 1878), who had made his fortune partly through the Chinese opium trade and founded the Far Eastern business empire of Jardine Matheson. The Gobelins tapestries were extensively damaged and had to be repaired in 1919 with partial reweavings.

As well as the Gobelins tapestries, in 1918 Lever also acquired the Mortlake tapestry series depicting the story of Hero and Leander, which had been sold from Stella Hall, near Newcastle, by the family of the industrialist Sir Joseph Cowen (1800–1873). The set may have been woven for the Hall (demolished in 1955), which in the 17th century was the home of the Tempests, a wealthy Catholic courtier family, loyal throughout the reigns of the Stuart kings when the Mortlake tapestry works was at the height of its fame and production.

**Tapestry**
French (Gobelins), c.1730–40
*The Report: The Month of July*
Woven in wool and silk;
425.5 x 353.5 cm
Purchased by Lever from Lews
Castle, Stornoway, 1918;
inv. no. LL 5203 (WHL 3539)

A French copy, woven to a reduced format and in reverse, of one of the prestigious series of twelve 16th-century Brussels tapestries which use hawking, deer- and boar-hunting scenes to represent months of the year. The series was collectively titled *The Hunts of Maximilian* (it may originally have been produced for the Emperor Charles V) and the Lady Lever Art Gallery owns tapestries representing three of the months, June, July and October. The copies were probably woven for an aristocrat at the court of Louis XV. The foreground hunters are making a 'report' of the animals of which they have found trace before setting off on the stag hunt. The figure on the horse to whom the hunters address their 'report' was previously thought to represent Mary of Hungary, sister of Charles V and Regent of the Low Countries, but it is now thought more likely to be her brother, Ferdinand of Austria. In the background is the Priory of Rouge-Cloître (Rooklooster), on the edge of the royal hunting forest of Soignes, south of Brussels, where the Emperor and his party often stopped during hunts.

**Tapestry**
English (Mortlake), *c.*1660–70
*The Meeting of Hero and Leander at the Temple of Venus, Sestos*
Woven in wool and silk;
286 x 311 cm approx. (sight size)
Purchased by Lever, 1918;
inv. no. LL 5464 (WHL 3604)

The Gallery owns a complete set of six of one of the most popular tapestry series woven at the Thames-side Mortlake tapestry works, illustrating the ancient Greek story of the tragic love of the priestess Hero for Leander. Leander swam the dangerous currents of the Hellespont, the straits between Europe and Asia at the Bosphorous, in order to see his love, but was drowned one stormy night. The series was designed by Mortlake's chief designer Francis Cleyn in 1625 and the first set was woven for James I. This set may have been woven for the Tempest family at Stella Hall, from where it was sold in 1918 (see p. 67).

The Mortlake works had been established in 1619 under royal patronage and made use of the weaving skills of immigrant Flemish workers. Their skill in depicting flesh is evident in the scene of *Leander's arrival at Hero's Tower* (right) in which Leander's naked body can be seen through the water.

**Embroidery**
**Damaris Pearse (1659–1679)**
English, c.1669–75
*The Drowning of Pharaoh in the Red Sea*
Satin embroidered with silk, metal thread, mica, and
seed pearls in a variety of stitches and knots including
long and short, split and padded detached buttonhole;
34 x 55.5 cm
Purchased by Lever, 1916; inv. no. LL 5229 (WHL 2795)

An example of a skillfully embroidered raised-work picture, in
which wooden moulds and wool padding were used to create
effects of three-dimensionality in some of the figures, while
others were worked on the surface of the satin to create a sense
of perspective. The picture was worked by a pious daughter of
a Nonconformist minister in Devon. He published a book in
memory of his daughter, *A Present for Youth and an Example for
the Aged: or the Remains of Damaris Pearse*, praising her Christian
virtues and her skill in 'the choicest sort of needleworks'.

**Casket**
British, dated 1667 and initialled H.P.
Canvas, satin and card faced onto a
wooden casket and embroidered with
silk, metal thread and seed pearls in a
variety of couched threads and surface
stitches including long and short, satin,
brick and padded detached buttonhole;
35.6 x 29.9 x 20.5 cm
Acquired by Lever before January 1907;
inv. no. LL 5256 (H 12)

The casket illustrates the Old Testament
story of the Sacrifice of Isaac, on the lid,
and three scenes from the meeting of
Isaac and Rebecca, around the sides.
The front drops to reveal slim velvet-
faced drawers, and the lid raises to
show a typical casket interior fitted
with a mirror, pincushion, bottles and
other compartments, including a central
mirrored well lined with a coloured
Flemish print of *David killing Goliath*
after an engraving of 1609 by Nicolas de
Bruyn.

## Embroidery

British, *c*.1768–1800
*Seated Shepherdess within a Floral Border*
Painted silk embroidered with silk in long
and short, satin, stem and speckling
stitches with French knots; 45 x 39.5 cm
Purchased by Lever, 1919;
inv. no. LL 5380 (WHL 3778)

The shepherdess may have been meant to
represent Leonora, with a pet robin on her
finger, from Isaac Bickerstaffe's popular
comedy *The Padlock*, first performed in
1768. The fine quality of the embroidery is
particularly evident in the elaborate floral
border.

## Gloves

English, *c*.1610–30
Leather with satin gauntlets,
stiffened with parchment
scraps, embroidered with silk in
satin stitch and metal thread
and trimmed with gold lace and
spangles;
length 35 x width 18 cm
Purchased by Lever, 1920;
inv. no. LL 5416 (X 3809)

The motifs embroidered on the
gauntlets (the part around the
wrist) – flaming hearts, eyes
weeping tears and pansies
representing sad thoughts –
suggest that the gloves may
have been intended to be
presented as a love token or a
*memento mori*. The gauntlets
have been stiffened with
parchment scraps made from
reused legal documents from
Norwich dating from 1602 or
earlier, suggesting that the
gloves date from soon
afterwards.

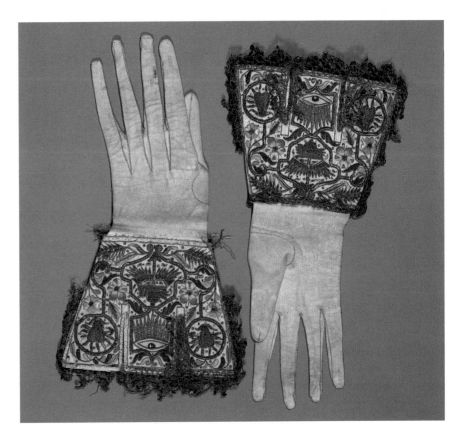

# chapter 4

# Wedgwood

The collection of Wedwood pottery includes the finest array in the world of the factory's most famous product, jasperware. The nucleus is an older collection, that of the 1st Lord Tweedmouth (1820–1894), which Lever purchased *en bloc* in 1905. Tweedmouth in turn had bought major pieces from the naturalist Charles Darwin, whose mother Susannah was a daughter of Josiah Wedgwood himself. He was one of the first to collect 18th-century Wedgwood, beginning in the late 1840s, and he arranged his collection at his house in Inverness-shire, Guisachan, for which he also commissioned a pioneering 'Adam revival' decorative scheme in the 1850s–60s from the London cabinet-makers Wright & Mansfield.

Lever's purchase of the Tweedmouth collection turned him into a major Wedgwood collector overnight (Fig. 13). The leading dealer in 'old Wedgwood' was Frederick Rathbone, and between 1905 and Rathbone's death in 1918, Lever used him to develop the collection into a thoroughly comprehensive one. Lever was prepared to back his own judgement against that of Rathbone, notably when the dealer advised against buying the group of plaques painted by Stubbs (see p. 25). Lever was buying at a time when important Victorian collections of 'old Wedgwood' were being dispersed, and wealthy Americans were entering the field. He was one of the very few British collectors of Wedgwood who had the resources to compete with them.

Josiah Wedgwood (1730–1795) stands unrivalled as the greatest English potter. He not only invented and developed new types of ware, but turned humble pottery into an item of fashionable taste, and exploited every opportunity of opening up new markets for his products. He first made his fortune in the 1760s with cream-coloured earthenware for the table, and continued to produce 'useful ware' of this kind as the bedrock of his business. At the same time he saw the potential for purely decorative 'ornamental ware' as part of the most up-to-date interior decoration. This was far beyond the ambitions of previous Staffordshire potters.

It is easy to miss the novelty of Wedgwood's 'ornamental ware' because its classical style is now all too familiar. But it was precisely this style, based on Greek and Roman art, that made it so novel in its own time. For many Georgian connoisseurs classical art provided 'the one true style' for serious works of art, and in the 1760s Robert Adam and other architects began to adapt this style – which they called the 'antique taste' – for interior decoration. The fashion was fuelled by the publication of exciting new archaeological discoveries, notably that of the buried cities of Herculaneum and Pompeii. Greek vases, thought at that time to be not Greek but Etruscan, were dug out of tombs and lavishly illustrated in the catalogue of Sir William Hamilton's collection in 1767. Wedgwood therefore named his new factory for decorative wares 'Etruria', carefully aiming its products at the market for interior decoration in the antique taste.

To attract this market Wedgwood needed the help of someone with a thorough knowledge of up-to-date interior design and of its ancient Greek and

Fig. 13 Wedgwood from the Tweedmouth collection displayed at The Hill, Lever's house in Hampstead, c.1910. In Lord Tweedmouth's time most of the collection was displayed at Guisachan in Inverness-shire, but this chimneypiece was at Brook House, Park Lane. All the Wedgwood items shown here are now in the Lady Lever Art Gallery, including the Stubbs self-portrait (painted on a Wedgwood plaque) hanging above the chimneypiece (see p. 25).

Roman sources. Shortly before production began at Etruria in 1769, he persuaded his close friend Thomas Bentley, a cosmopolitan Liverpool merchant with a background in textile dealing, to go into partnership with him. With Bentley Wedgwood produced 'ornamental ware', while he had another partnership with his cousin Thomas Wedgwood for producing 'useful ware'. Bentley suggested products, briefed designers and watched London society for the latest trends to enable the firm to keep ahead of its competitors. The Lady Lever collection consists almost entirely of the 'ornamental ware' produced by Wedgwood and Bentley until the latter's death in 1780 and afterwards in the name of Wedgwood alone.

The principal products made by the partnership in its first three or four years were vases decorated to resemble agate, veined marble and other stones. The shiny, glazed surface which was normal on Staffordshire earthenware was perfectly suited to them. But unglazed stoneware seemed more suitable for evoking the semi-matt surface of ancient pottery and the delicacy of carved reliefs, and Wedgwood spent the rest of his life perfecting different coloured stonewares of this type. First was the black, which he called 'basaltes' after the basalt rock used for sculpture. Caneware, which is cane-coloured, and 'rosso antico' ('ancient red') were also developed.

The jasperware for which Wedgwood is famous above all else is a white, slightly translucent stoneware (Wedgwood sometimes called it a porcelain), which could take an even tint of one of various colours. By 1774 blue and green were successful, to be followed later by lilac and yellow. Jasperware was inspired by cameo carvings in hardstones or shell, in which one colour of material is cut away around the design to reveal another colour below as the background. Jasperware could be made, however, on a much larger scale, and brought the delicacy of jewellery to interior decoration. Jasper was at first coloured right through the body, but Wedgwood rapidly developed the ability to achieve an even finish with a thin layer of coloured jasper over a white jasper body. This 'jasper dip' saved on the quantity of colouring agents needed for each piece. The through-coloured 'solid jasper' continued to be used for some of the best pieces where density of colour was required.

After Wedgwood's death in 1795 the factory lost its great innovative dynamo. When fashion swung away from classicism in the 1820s, the firm fell on hard times. Its fortunes were revived around the time of the Great Exhibition of 1851, but by then pioneer collectors like the future Lord Tweedmouth were already collecting 'old Wedgwood'.

**Vase**
*c.*1775
White terracotta stoneware decorated with underglaze oxides, and gilding;
28 x 17.1 x dia. 12.8 cm
Purchased by Lever from the Tweedmouth collection, 1905; inv. no. LL 1018 (H 428)

Vases of this type were the principal product of the early years of the Wedgwood and Bentley partnership. For twenty years Staffordshire potters had imitated marble by using coloured oxides which ran in the glaze. Wedgwood's innovation was to use this technique for vases in the 'antique taste' fashionable for interior decoration. 'Terracotta stoneware' was Wedgwood's term for the type of body used here.
This vase is fixed to its plinth with a screw, and the plinth is marked 'Wedgwood and Bentley Etruria' in a circle around the screw-hole. Wedgwood was the first British potter regularly to mark his wares with the name of the firm.

**The Callipygian Venus**
*c.*1775
Black basalt; 38 x 30 cm
Purchased by Lever from
Frederick Rathbone, 1916;
inv. no. LL 1397 (X 1785)

The basalt frame is integral, and the background is painted in the matt colour which Wedgwood called 'encaustic'. The figure copies an ancient statue which was very popular with visitors to Rome in the 18th century. Its title means 'with a beautiful bottom' and it was connected with a legend told by the Greek writer Athenaeus. Two sisters solved a dispute over whose bottom was the more beautiful by asking a young man unknown to both of them to choose. His reward was the girl of his choice.

**Vase**

*c.*1785
Black basalt; 30.9 x dia. 14.4 cm
Purchased by Lever from
Frederick Rathbone, 1917;
inv. no. LL 1148 (X 1792)

Wedgwood patented the matt, fired
colours that he named 'encaustic',
which he used on black basalt to
imitate Greek red-figure vase
painting (see p. 95). An attempt to
prosecute his competitor
Humphrey Palmer for infringing
his patent was, however,
unsuccessful. The technique was
used on the 'First Day's vases',
which Josiah made on the wheel on
the first day of production at Etruria
in 1769. It was quite different from
the ancient 'encaustic' painting
technique described by the Roman
writer Pliny, but since there was
learned controversy about this in
Wedgwood's time, he chose it as a
stylish brand name.

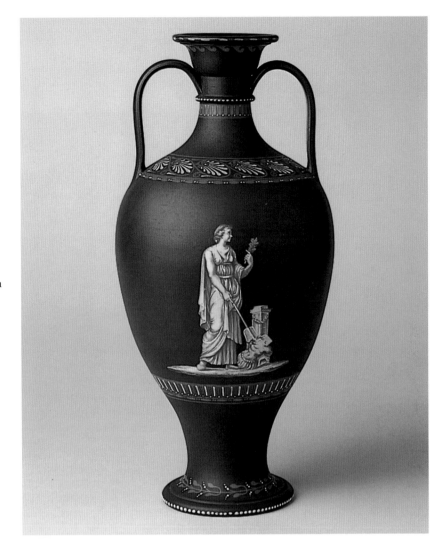

**Figures of Cupid and Psyche**
**After Etienne-Maurice Falconet**
**(1716–1791)**
*c.*1780–1800
Black basalt; 19.9 x 10.7 x 14.5 cm,
19.9 x 10.5 x 11.7 cm
Purchased by Lever from the
Tweedmouth collection, 1905;
inv. nos. LL 1130, LL 1129
(H 430, H 429)

The 'antique taste' made small
bronze figures increasingly popular
as furnishing for rooms.
Wedgwood's black basalt provided
a cheaper alternative which
resembled bronze with a dark
patina. Falconet, who was director
of sculpture at the French royal
porcelain factory of Sèvres, made
these figures first in marble in 1757
and then in biscuit (that is,
unglazed) porcelain the following
year. Wedgwood may have copied
them from the Sèvres version or
from a plaster cast.

**Chimneypiece**

*c*.1786

Marble set with tablets of blue jasper with white jasper reliefs; 160.5 x 207.6 x (depth from wall) 19.5 cm
Purchased by Lever from Moss Harris & Sons, 1920; inv. no. LL 2643 (X 3767)

In 1777 Wedgwood wrote that Mr Heathcote was enquiring after chimneypiece tablets for Longton Hall. This and another similar chimneypiece in the collection come from this house, but both are likely to date from a few years later. It was 1786 when Wedgwood wrote that he was making six chimneypieces of a new type, with even the jamb or upright panels made of jasper. The central tablet here is *The Apotheosis of Virgil* which was modelled by Flaxman as a pair to his *Apotheosis of Homer*. The three chimneypieces of this type in the Lady Lever Art Gallery are the only ones in any public collection.

**Bust of Homer**

*c*.1790

Black basalt 'bronzed' (painted); 55.7 x 30.1 x 28.4 cm
Purchased by Lever from Frederick Rathbone, 1918; inv. no. LL 1109 (X 2569)

In 1774 Wedgwood and Bentley bought from John Cheere at Hyde Park Corner a plaster cast of a bust of Homer for 10s 6d. This was probably the origin of the present model, but its ultimate source is an ancient bust now in the National Museum at Naples. Bronze busts were a favoured decoration for libraries, where they were ranged along the tops of bookcases. Cheere sold plaster busts not only in the white, but also painted to resemble bronze. Wedgwood used a similar technique on basalt, but the original finish has almost invariably been lost; this bust is a rare exeption.

**Wax relief**
**Giuseppe Angelini (1742–1811)**
1789
*Geniuses representing the Pleasures of the*
*Elysian Fields*
Wax on slate; 16.5 x 40.5 cm (sight size)
Purchased by Lever from the Tweedmouth
collection, 1905; inv. no. LL 2660 (H 389)

Between 1788 and 1790 Wedgwood commissioned some thirty wax models
to be made in Rome, copying ancient relief sculptures in the Capitoline
Museum. He was able to use the illustrations in a recently published
catalogue of the Museum collection as a guide. This model was made by
Giuseppe Angelini copying a Roman funerary urn. For a jasper version see
the flower pot below. The Elysian Fields were believed to be the home of
the blessed in the afterlife.

**Flower pot**
*c.*1790
Lilac jasper dip with white
jasper reliefs; 10.3 x 26 x 13.3 cm
Purchased by Lever from the
Tweedmouth collection, 1905;
inv. no. LL 1171 (H 472)

Lilac jasper was mentioned by
Bentley in a letter to
Wedgwood, but most seems to
have been made after Bentley's
death in 1780. The colour was
difficult to control, and was
therefore more commonly used
for small pieces. This pair of
pots for flowers or 'roots' can be
dated by their relief decoration.
The wax model by Giuseppe
Angelini from which it is taken
(see above) was received by
Wedgwood in March 1790.
Wedgwood was careful to
distinguish between pots for
holding plants and vases for the
chimneypiece, which were not
expected to hold anything.

**Plaque**
**Designed by John Flaxman**
**(1755–1826)**
*c.*1790
*Peace preventing Mars from opening the*
*Door of the Temple of Janus*
Solid blue jasper with white jasper
reliefs; 22.8 x 25 cm (sight size)
Purchased by Lever from Frederick
Rathbone, 1918;
inv. no. LL 1691 (X 2415)

In ancient Rome the door of the temple
of Janus was opened when war was
declared. Bentley selected Flaxman to
model relief designs for the firm in
1775. The subject of this relief was
chosen to celebrate the Commercial
Treaty of 1786 with France. For his
original wax model (now in the
Wegwood Museum at Barlaston)
Flaxman was paid fifteen guineas in
January 1787. By this time his practice
as a sculptor was flourishing, and
modelling for Wedgwood was taking
second place. After he left for Rome
later in the year, Flaxman's work for
Wedgwood was virtually over.

**'Borghese' vases and pedestals**
*c.*1790 and later
Solid blue jasper with white jasper
reliefs; each vase 50.3 x 27.5 cm,
each pedestal 31.5 x 26.7 cm
Purchased by Lever from the
Tweedmouth collection, 1905;
inv. nos. LL 1023–1026 (H 540–541)

These vases, the largest Josiah
Wedgwood ever made in jasper, bear
relief decoration following a wax model
made by John Devaere in Rome in 1788.
Devaere was copying the reliefs on the
Borghese Vase, regarded by 18th-
century critics as, with the Medici vase,
one of the two finest ancient marble
vases in existence. While the relief
decoration of Wedgwood's vases
follows closely that of the original, their
form does not. The Borghese Vase is
now in the Louvre in Paris.

**Copy of the Portland Vase**
*c*.1790
Solid black jasper with white jasper reliefs;
25.6 x dia. 18.5 cm
Purchased by Lever from the Tweedmouth
collection, 1905; inv. no. LL 1204 (H 527)

The ancient Roman glass vase known as the
Portland Vase is now in the British Museum. It
was bought from the Barberini family in Rome
and sold to Sir William Hamilton in 1783.
Hamilton brought it to England and sold it to
the Duchess of Portland. Three years later
Wedgwood borrowed the vase from the Duke
of Portland in order to copy it in jasper. He was
a man of his time in regarding the meticulous
imitation of a classical work as his finest
achievement. Wedgwood's copy went on
display in 1790, but probably only about thirty-
five of this 'first edition' were made.

**Cup and saucer**
*c*.1800
Green jasper dip with white and lilac jasper reliefs;
cup 7 x 9.5 x 6.8 cm; saucer 2.4 x dia. 12 cm
Purchased by Lever from Frederick Rathbone, 1917;
inv. nos. LL 1333–1334 (X 2180)

Jasper in three colours appears to have been in production by 1786.
Wedgwood's distinction between 'ornamental' and 'useful' wares was
never very watertight, and the ceramic bodies of which they were made
played an important part. Anything made of jasper tended to be
regarded as 'ornamental'. Jasper was used, however for the delicate
little tea or coffee services for one or two persons, known as 'dejeuners',
which were used by the wealthy in their dressing-rooms.

**Part of a tea service**
*c*.1805
Caneware; teapot 10.8 x 19.8 x 12.3 cm,
sugarbowl 7.5 x dia. 12 cm,
cup 6.4 x 10.8 x dia. 8.9 cm,
saucer 2.9 x dia. 14.7 cm
Purchased by Lever from Frederick Rathbone,
1916;inv. nos. LL 1088–1093 (X 961)

Wedgwood was making a cane-coloured
stoneware experimentally in 1771, but had
problems with the body staining and does not
seem to have been satisfied with it until some
years later. The caneware body was not
generally used for large tablets or vases, but
was employed for figures and for vessels like
plant pots. The first teaware made in it was
probably that moulded to imitate bamboo
canes. After Josiah's death in 1795 the body
was employed for a wider range of wares.

# chapter 5

# Chinese Art

Chinese porcelain was one of Lever's greatest enthusiasms as a collector, which he had already embraced by the mid-1890s and sustained to the end of his life. He particularly admired the 'blue and white' and the enamelled (mainly 'famille verte') wares of the Kangxi period (1662–1722), and it is these that dominate the Gallery's Chinese holdings. The major exception to the British concentration of the Gallery's collections, Chinese porcelain was likewise a prominent feature of the collection of James Orrock, whose championship of British art was so influential on the course of Lever's own collecting: it would seem that both men considered such 'china' to be an essential component of British taste in the 17th and 18th centuries and thus suitable for a collection devoted to British art and decoration of that period. However, the taste for 'blue and white' was also, at the start of Lever's collecting career, an important aspect of the Aesthetic Movement, and was promoted by artists such as D.G. Rossetti, J.A.M. Whistler and Frederic Leighton, as well as by other wealthy collectors.

Lever himself was always a conservative collector, whose taste in this field scarcely changed between the 1890s, when he began collecting Chinese porcelain for Thornton Manor (see Fig. 14), and his death thirty years later. However, after deciding to establish the Lady Lever Art Gallery in 1913, he broadened the scope of his purchases to include items of more general interest: carved hardstones (see p. 91), cloisonné enamels (see p. 85), painted glass pictures (see p. 93), and Ming dynasty 'fahua' ceramics (see p. 84). But, with the exception of a Han dynasty pot bought in 1916, he ignored the new interest in early Chinese art that developed after about 1906. After Lever's death in 1925, the Trustees of the Gallery acquired a few examples of Han, Tang and Song dynasty wares in order to provide a wider-ranging view of Chinese ceramic history.

Lever's habit of buying wholesale from well-known collections was a major factor in the formation of his collection of Chinese art – a field in which he doubtless judged it safer to draw on the expertise of others. The most spectacular instance of this practice came in 1911 when he agreed to pay, by installments, the prodigious sum of £275,000 for the highly-regarded collection of Richard Bennett, a fellow Bolton industrialist (see pp. 86, 89). Problems arose when Lever's supposedly secret part in the deal was leaked, and he repudiated the purchase; but after two years of legal wrangling with the dealer Edgar Gorer, Lever agreed to retain fifty-one items from the collection, for £55,000. Among these were two exceptionally fine 'prunus' jars and several pieces of 'famille noire' (see pp. 88–9) – two types of porcelain that had by then become highly fashionable, and exceedingly expensive. While prestige must have had a lot to do with Lever's interest in the Bennett collection, after 1913 this type of 'bulk buying' became a convenient way of acquiring for his museum representative selections of good-quality objects that lay outside his main area of interest. Thus, all his jade carvings and cloisonné enamels came from just two sources: the famous collection of Sir Trevor Lawrence (in 1916; see p. 91) and that of Lord Wharncliffe (in 1920). Other collections from which Lever bought Chinese art *en bloc* were those of Sydney E. Kennedy (see pp. 84, 89), Alfred W. Stiff (see p. 85), Robert H. Benson and, in 1903

Fig. 14 One end of the Music Room at Thornton Manor, 1903. (RCHME © Crown Copyright)

and 1904, James Orrock (Lever's later bulk-purchases from Orrock included very little Chinese material).

The kind of porcelain that had been so admired by Europeans in the 17th and 18th centuries, and which is so well represented in Lever's collection, was made almost exclusively in private factories at Jingdezhen, China's main ceramics centre in the southern central province of Jiangxi. From the early 17th century (the late Ming dynasty) onwards, huge quantities of 'blue and white' were produced specifically for export to Europe. This type of ware is decorated with a cobalt oxide pigment before it is glazed; the object, its decoration and its glaze are all fired together in one high-temperature firing that turns the cobalt oxide bright blue (before firing it is almost black). Enamelled porcelain, also largely designed for export, was produced in quantity from at least the beginning of the Qing dynasty in 1644. These wares are fired twice: first, the object (either glazed or unglazed) is fired at a high temperature; next, it is painted with enamel colours either on the glaze or on the 'biscuit' (the unglazed porcelain body); finally, it is fired again at a lower temperature to fuse the enamels to the surface. Following a scheme devised in 1862 by the French collector Albert Jacquemart, enamelled wares have generally been classified in the West according to the predominant colour – 'famille verte', 'famille jaune', 'famille noire', 'famille rose' (the green, yellow, black and pink 'families'). This is, however, a system that the Chinese themselves have never used. Because both blue and white and enamelled porcelains were designed for a foreign market, their decoration tends to reflect not so much Chinese aesthetic values as those of Europeans with a romanticized view of China.

Much, but by no means all, Chinese porcelain bears a mark of some kind. The nature of the marks used varies according to the manufacturer and the purpose of the vessel. From the early Ming dynasty onwards virtually all official wares, produced by the imperial factories for use by the emperor and his court, bore the reign mark. These marks usually consist of six characters and feature the reign title of the ruling emperor (Kangxi, for example). The use of marks became more complicated in the Qing dynasty. This was partly the result of a decree of 1677, which banned the use of the reign mark to avoid dishonour to the imperial name if a vessel should be broken. The decree was quickly either ignored or revoked, but seems to have encouraged the habit of using a variety of other mark types. For example, auspicious symbols are commonly found, such as the artemisia leaf (a protection against diseases: see p. 87) and the sacred *lingzhi* fungus (a symbol of long life: see p. 88). It also became fashionable to use the reign marks of earlier periods, most commonly those of Xuande (1426–1435), Chenghua (1465–1487) (see pp. 87, 88) and Jiajing (1522–1566). These marks were not intended to deceive the buyer but to show respect for what were considered to be the greatest periods of porcelain production. Vessels which bear alternative marks of these kinds – and some which bear the contemporary imperial reign mark – were produced by non-imperial commercial factories.

One of the first Europeans to come across Chinese porcelain was Marco Polo (1254–1324). It seems that he also gave it its European name when he called it *porcellana*, an Italian word for cowrie shell. Before the end of the 16th century porcelain was an extreme rarity in Europe, much admired and very expensive. The thinness, translucency and smooth, hard, white surface of this treasured material made it seem vastly superior to the coarse, brown native earthenware and stoneware, and owners often had their porcelain vessels elaborately mounted in silver. The fact that the secret of porcelain's manufacture was unknown in Europe added to its magical qualities and encouraged the quest to reproduce it. Artificial (or 'soft-paste') porcelain, using different ingredients from the Chinese, was produced in Florence between 1575 and 1587 by Duke Francesco I de' Medici and more successfully in France from about 1673. True 'hard-paste' porcelain is made from two ingredients, kaolin (china clay) and the related material petuntse (china stone). The secret of its composition was only discovered in 1708 or 1709, by the German alchemist Johann Friedrich Böttger, while employed at Meissen in Germany by Augustus the Strong, Elector of Saxony. Porcelain mania swept Europe in the 18th century. Production was dominated at first by Meissen, then from the middle of the century by the soft-paste porcelain of Sèvres in France and of such factories as Chelsea, Bow and Worcester in England. By the early 19th century the cheaper European products had largely replaced porcelain imported from China. Nevertheless, Jingdezhen continued to export its goods to Europe and from the 1870s western collectors developed a renewed enthusiasm for the antique and contemporary porcelain of east Asia.

After about 1910 wealthy collectors competed with each other for possession of 'famille noire' porcelain. Extravagantly high prices were paid and it was almost inevitable that forgeries found their way onto the market. A genuine piece of 'famille noire' is basically the same as 'famille verte' ware: the design is painted on in enamel colours, which are then fired at a relatively low temperature to fix them. The difference is that in 'famille verte' porcelain the background is usually left unpainted (and therefore white), while on 'famille noire' pieces the background is filled in with a series of enamels, which accumulate to form a dense black. Because the surface of the pot is completely covered, the black ground can be applied either on the biscuit or over the glaze. It is therefore possible to take a genuine piece of early 'famille verte' porcelain and give it a fresh black ground, and it is clear that this often happened at the height of 'famille noire' fever. Lever bought 'famille noire' with as much care as he could, fully aware of the risk of mistakes. Even so, the question of which 'famille noire' pieces in his collection are genuinely early is still open to debate.

Until the mid-19th century, exported Chinese porcelain came to Europe mainly in the ships of the English and Dutch East India Companies. The main official trade was in tea, silk and porcelain bought in bulk, but a wide range of goods was traded privately as a profitable sideline for the individual merchants involved. The unofficial trade was dominated by luxury porcelain but also included paintings on mirrored glass, perhaps the only export product that did not develop from an existing domestic industry (see p. 93). In 1834 the English East India Company lost its monopoly of the China trade, and after 1842 Britain, having won the First Opium War, opened China to all western traders by force of arms. China's artistic heritage now began to drain away overseas, removed from temples, palaces and tombs by western dealers or their agents, often in dubious circumstances. This may be how Lever's cloisonné enamel altar vessels (see p. 85) and the Gallery's important stoneware figure of Guanyin (see p. 84) first came to Europe.

The collection of Chinese art formed by Lever was never intended to be comprehensive, but primarily to bring him private pleasure and to complement his holdings of 18th-century British art; in comparison with other collections being assembled by the end of his life it was distinctly old-fashioned. It is, nevertheless, distinguished by a number of particularly interesting individual pieces, and by the standards of connoisseurship of his day it is outstanding.

## A selective Chinese chronology

| | | | |
|---|---|---|---|
| HAN DYNASTY | 206 B.C. – A.D. 220 | | |
| TANG DYNASTY | A.D. 618 – 906 | Longqing reign | 1567 – 1572 |
| SONG DYNASTY | 960 – 1279 | Wanli reign | 1573 – 1620 |
| YUAN DYNASTY | 1279 – 1368 | Taichang reign | 1620 |
| MING DYNASTY | 1368 – 1644 | Tianqi reign | 1621 – 1627 |
| Xuande reign | 1426 – 1435 | Chongzhen reign | 1628 – 1644 |
| Zhengtong reign | 1436 – 1449 | QING DYNASTY | 1644 – 1911 |
| Jingtai reign | 1450 – 1456 | Shunzhi reign | 1644 – 1661 |
| Tianshun reign | 1457 – 1464 | Kangxi reign | 1662 – 1722 |
| Chenghua reign | 1465 – 1487 | Yongzheng reign | 1723 – 1735 |
| Hongzhi reign | 1488 – 1505 | Qianlong reign | 1736 – 1795 |
| Zhengde reign | 1506 – 1521 | Jiaqing reign | 1796 – 1820 |
| Jiajing reign | 1522 – 1566 | Daoguang reign | 1821 – 1850 |

**Vase**
Southern China, Ming dynasty, *c.*1475–1500
Porcelain enamelled on the biscuit in the 'fahua' style;
42 x dia. 27 cm
Purchased by Lever from the Sydney E. Kennedy sale,
1916; inv. no. LL 6067 (X 1529)

The 'fahua' style of ceramics was produced in China
from the 14th to 16th centuries and may well have
been intended as a less expensive substitute for
cloisonné enamels. The bold designs on this type of pot
are outlined with threads of clay; after firing, the
outlined areas are filled in with a limited range of
coloured glazes. The origin of the term 'fahua' is
uncertain but it may mean 'Buddhist decoration' and
derive from the fact that these wares were very often
used in Buddhist temples. This vase features the so-
called Eight Immortals of the Wine Cup, a group of
poets of the Tang dynasty (618–906) 'immortalized' in
the work of the poet Du Fu (712–770) and as famous
for their drunkenness as for their verse. Their faces
have been left unglazed and they are identified by the
wine jars that they are leaning on.

**Figure of Guanyin**
**Liu Zhen**
Northern China, Chenghua reign (1465–1487), 1484
Stoneware with coloured glazes;
140 x 73.3 x 48 cm
Purchased by the 2nd Viscount Leverhulme, *c.*1937;
presented to the Gallery by the 3rd Viscount
Leverhulme, 1980; inv. no. LL 6000

Guanyin is the Chinese (and normally female)
manifestation of the Buddhist Bodhisattva of
compassion, Avalokitesvara. Bodhisattvas are beings
who have reached Nirvana (Enlightenment) but who
choose to stay in the world to help others achieve the
same. An inscription on this figure tells us that it was
the gift of a man named Dang and his wife Chong,
dedicated on an auspicious mid-autumn day in 1484
under the supervision of the priest Daoji. It belongs to
a group of at least four different figures from the same
unknown northern Chinese temple, all dedicated on
the same occasion and inscribed with the maker's
name, Liu Zhen. The group, now split up between
various British museums, appears to have been taken
from China in the 1930s, when the 2nd Viscount
Leverhulme (and not his father) acquired the Guanyin.

**Peach-shaped wine pot**
Ming dynasty, c.1575–1600
Porcelain with coloured glazes;
15.7 x 17.3 x 10.5 cm
Purchased by Lever from from the Alfred W.
Stiff sale, 1916; inv. no. LL 23 (X 1680)

The peach is an important symbol of long life,
sacred to the Daoist goddess Xiwang Mu (the
Queen Mother of the West). The peaches of
longevity grow in her garden in the Kunlun
Mountains and are the main delicacy at her
birthday banquets. Hence, peaches are
commonly found in association with birthday
gifts and are popular among Daoists, for whom
the quest for immortality is of central
importance. This type of wine pot, which has
no lid and is filled through a hole in the base,
was copied by several English potters in the
form of 'Cadogan' teapots, which were
particularly popular in the years around 1830.

**Beaker**
Ming dynasty, probably Wanli reign
(1573–1620), c.1600
Cloisonné enamel on copper;
56.3 x 39.9 x 39.8 cm
Purchased by Lever from the Alfred W. Stiff
sale, 1916; inv. no. LL 5901 (X 1486)

After Chinese connoisseurs began to collect
archaic bronze vessels in the Tang dynasty
(618–906), it became common to imitate bronze
forms in other materials. The form of this
vessel is not genuinely archaic but is made to
appear so by the addition of four cast ribs to
the sides. The beaker is one of a pair and would
originally have been accompanied by an
incense burner and two candlesticks to form a
temple altar set. The Buddhist decoration of
scrolling lotus flowers symbolizes
Enlightenment. The cloisonné enamel
technique involves soldering a pattern of wires
onto a metal surface; the enclosed areas
(cloisons) are filled with enamel colours which
are then fired and polished to create a smooth,
sparkling surface. On the base of this beaker is
a Jingtai reign mark (1450–1456), paying
homage to what the Chinese consider to have
been the classic period for this art form.
Although technical perfection was achieved in
the Qing dynasty (1644–1911), the bolder forms
and richer colours of the earlier period
compare favourably with the fussier, more
glittery style of the 18th and 19th centuries.

**Two figures of Kuixing**
(left) Ming dynasty (1368–1644), *c.*1600–1644
Porcelain with coloured glazes;
30.5 x 22.1 x 10.7 cm
Purchased by Lever, 1916;
inv. no. LL 6134 (X 1697)

(right) Kangxi reign (1662–1722), *c.*1662–1700
Porcelain enamelled on the biscuit in 'famille
verte' colours; 32 x 22.2 x 11.5 cm
Purchased by Lever, 1915;
inv. no. LL 61 (X 442)

In Chinese popular religion, Kuixing is the patron of students who
awards success in examinations. Standing on a fish-dragon, he holds up
a writing brush in his right hand and an inkstone in his left hand. He is
said to have been an historical figure, a poor but brilliant student called
Zhong Kui who passed the imperial examinations with high honours.
However, because he was repulsively ugly (as these figures show), he
was not allowed to enter government service. In despair, he drowned
himself but was carried by a fish-dragon up to heaven where he became
a star ('xing' in Chinese) in the Great Bear constellation (known in China
as the Palace of Literary Genius). Although these two figures are closely
similar in form, the one on the right, decorated in the 'famille verte'
manner, was made somewhat later than the one on the left.

**Wine ewer**
Kangxi reign (1662–1722), *c.*1662–1700
Porcelain enamelled on the biscuit in 'famille verte' colours;
22.6 x 20.4 x 5.6 cm
Purchased by Lever from the Richard Bennett collection, 1911–13;
inv. no. LL 24 (RB 283)

This ewer is modelled in the form of the character 'shou', meaning 'long
life'. The panels on each side underline this symbolism. On one side can
be seen four symbols of longevity: a pine tree, a crane, a deer and the
sacred 'lingzhi' fungus. On the other side (shown here) two cranes are
flying towards a pavilion.

**Plate**
Kangxi reign (1662–1722), *c*.1662–1700
Porcelain enamelled over the glaze in
'famille verte' colours, with some gilding;
5.4 x dia. 37.6 cm
Acquired by Lever before June 1907;
inv. no. LL 32 (H 15)

Two mounted warriors are engaged in
combat, perhaps an historical subject
derived from a contemporary illustrated
book. The rim decoration includes
medallions containing cranes, emblems
of long life. On the back, the plate has
flowers painted over an incised petal
pattern. There are two marks: a non-
imperial factory mark of an artemisia
leaf, an auspicious plant said to drive
away diseases; and a later engraved mark
of the collection of Augustus the Strong,
Elector of Saxony. Presumably the plate
was once displayed in the Japanese
Palace built for Augustus in Dresden
between 1729 and 1737. Augustus was a
notoriously extravagant collector of east
Asian porcelain; on one occasion he is
said to have given away a whole
regiment of dragoons in exchange for
twelve Chinese vases.

**Dish**
Kangxi reign (1662–1722),
*c*.1700–22
Porcelain enamelled over the glaze
in 'famille verte' colours, with
some gilding; 3.5 x dia. 26.7 cm
Acquired by Lever before June
1907; inv. no. LL 68 (H 283)

Three heroes of 'The Water
Margin', the popular novel written
in the 16th century by Shi Nai'an,
are identified by the names on their
belts: (left to right) Chai Jin, Song
Jiang and Yan Qing. The figures
are probably based on illustrations
of the novel made by Chen
Hongshou in the 1640s and 1650s.
Similar dishes with different heroes
exist in other collections. Although
the dish was made during the
Kangxi reign, it has on the base a
mark of the Chenghua reign
(1465–1487). This mark is not
intended to deceive but to show
respect for the excellent ceramics of
the earlier period; it is also a sign
that the dish was made by a non-
imperial factory (see p. 82).

**Pair of vases**
Kangxi reign (1662–1722)
Porcelain enamelled over the glaze in 'famille verte' colours; 43.8 x dia. 20.9 cm
Acquired by Lever before June 1907;
inv. nos. LL 28, LL 6110 (H 240)

These vases depict the 'Four Elegant Accomplishments', cultural pursuits traditionally considered to be appropriate for women of leisure and scholars. On one vase, Painting is represented by three women looking at a picture scroll and Literature by a woman reading at a table. The other vase features Games (women playing checkers) and Music (a woman playing a 'qin', a zither-like stringed instrument). The landscapes round the neck are probably the work of a different specialist painter. On the base of each vase is painted a sacred fungus; this is the mark of a private, non-imperial factory and expresses a wish for long life.

**Vase**
Probably Kangxi reign (1662–1722)
Porcelain enamelled on the biscuit in 'famille noire' colours; 76.2 x dia. 27.1 cm
Acquired by Lever before June 1907;
inv. no. LL 6130 (H 259)

Lever insured this vase for £10,000, a reflection of the fact that 'famille noire' became, in the 1910s and '20s, the most sought-after and expensive porcelain in the world. Although these wares are usually rather crudely decorated, prices shot up to unprecedented levels. It is now suspected that much of the 'famille noire' sold at this time was either faked or produced by adding a black ground to genuine 'famille verte' items. Lever himself was aware of this problem and always preferred to examine pieces in person before buying. It has been suggested that pieces of 'famille noire' as big as this could not have been made as early as the Kangxi reign, but this vase does in fact seem to be a genuine early example. It has a Chenghua reign mark (1465–1487), a sign that it was made by a non-imperial factory.

**Candle-holder**
Kangxi reign (1662–1722)
Porcelain enamelled over the glaze in 'famille
noire' and 'famille verte' colours;
41 x 26.2 x 16.3 cm
Purchased by Lever from the Sydney E.
Kennedy sale, 1916; inv. no. LL 6131 (X 1550)

A young African woman holds in her right hand a
horn-shaped candle socket. Her elaborate jewellery
includes real pearl earrings, a star-shaped
ornament on her forehead and a sash of flowers. By
the time that this unusual figure was made the
Chinese had been familiar with Africans for many
centuries; there were African slaves in China as
early as the Tang dynasty (618–906), and between
1405 and 1433 seven major maritime expeditions,
led by the Muslim eunuch Zheng He, had reached
the east coast of Africa. By the Kangxi period a
large African community was established in the
Portuguese settlement at Macao. Lever's collection
contains another similar candle-holder bought on a
separate occasion.

**Jar and lid**
Kangxi reign (1662–1722), *c.*1700
Porcelain with underglaze blue decoration;
26.2 x dia. 21.8 cm
Purchased by Lever from the Richard Bennett
collection, 1911–13; inv. no. LL 72 (RB 1)

'Prunus' jars like this became an obsession of
British and American collectors in the late 1890s
and by 1905 could sell for up to £6000 each.
Connoisseurs paid attention to the perfection of the
azure blue colour and, according to those
standards, this example of Lever's has been
considered the finest in any western collection. The
jars were used in China as containers for gifts of tea
or other delicacies at the lunar New Year Festival
in January or February. Appropriately, the design
celebrates the approach of spring: branches of
prunus blossom (which appears in late winter) are
depicted against a background of cracking ice.

**Vase**
Kangxi reign (1662–1722), *c.*1700–22
Porcelain with underglaze blue decoration, enamelled over the glaze in 'famille verte' colours, with gilding;
43.8 x dia. 19.4 cm
Acquired by Lever before June 1907; inv. no. LL 93 (H 289)

Lever's enthusiasm was clearly aroused by the unusual 'powder blue' technique; this vase is just one example from the large collection he formed. The speckled ground was produced by blowing powdered cobalt oxide onto the unglazed pot through a bamboo tube with gauze over the end. The reserved white areas on this vase were masked by paper patches, applied in the slapdash manner often found on work intended for export. The white panels were then painted in 'famille verte' colours (fixed by a second low-temperature firing) with a design of black-backed finches sitting on prunus branches. The gilded design of plants, birds and insects on the blue ground has survived unusually well, considering how easily such gilding is rubbed off.

**Vase and lid**
Qianlong reign (1736–1795)
Porcelain with underglaze blue decoration;
31.8 x dia. 15.9 cm
Acquired by Lever before June 1907;
inv. no. LL 26 (H 159)

This vase was made at a time when blue and white porcelain was out of fashion in China. Nevertheless, it displays a lively and imaginative sense of design, with the gourds in the decoration neatly echoing the overall form of the vase. The double-gourd shape is a traditional Chinese form not usually found in wares made for export, suggesting that this vase may have been intended for the Chinese domestic market.

**Garniture of three lidded vases and two beakers**
Kangxi reign (1662–1722), *c*.1662–1700
Porcelain with underglaze blue decoration;
(left to right, height x diameter) 54.5 x 20.5 cm, 48.9 x 23.7 cm,
55.9 x 20.5 cm, 48.7 x 23.5 cm, 54.9 x 20.7 cm
Purchased by Lever from the George Salting sale, 1900;
inv. nos. LL 96–100 (H 53)

Blue and white groups of this sort decorated the walls, mantelpieces and furniture of wealthy Europeans in vast numbers from at least the middle of the 17th century. Lever followed firmly in this tradition and this garniture is typical of his personal taste. In the West, the design has been called the 'rose and ticket' pattern after the flowers round the sides and the ticket-like oval medallions round the rims or shoulders.

**Vase and lid**
Qing dynasty (1644–1911),
*c*.1780–1830
Jade (nephrite); 35.6 x 23 x 8.5 cm
Purchased by Lever from the Sir Trevor Lawrence sale, 1916;
inv. no. LL 70 (X 1425)

Made from one piece of jade, this vase displays the great virtuosity achieved by the best jade-carvers of the Qing dynasty; it may even have been made for imperial use. Jade is too hard to be cut with steel tools and therefore must be ground with abrasive sands and water, down to the smallest detail, a slow and very demanding process. In Chinese culture jade has always been more highly esteemed than gold, not only because the main source is far away in Central Asia but also because of the spiritual qualites it is believed to embody. This vase is an altar vessel and bears around the edge of each side the eight Buddhist Auspicious Signs: (clockwise from the top) the Umbrella, the Paired Fish, the Vase, the Lotus Flower, the Conch Shell, the Endless Knot, the Banner of Victory, and the Dharma Wheel (the wheel of Buddhist law, symbolizing the unity of all things).

**Altar ornament**
Qianlong reign (1736–1795)
Porcelain enamelled over the glaze in
'famille rose' colours, with jade, coral and
ivory; 70.6 x 63.6 x 39.8 cm
Purchased by Lever, 1920;
inv. no. LL 6133 (X 3830/1)

One of a pair of Buddhist altar ornaments
in the form of an elaborately-dressed
elephant. The elephant is a Chinese symbol
of peace and, in Buddhist thought, is
ridden by the Bodhisattva Samantabhadra.
A vase on its back is a symbolic container
for the three sacred Buddhist jewels – the
Buddha, the Dharma (the Buddha's
teachings) and the Sangha (the community
of practising Buddhists). The vase on this
elephant is painted to imitate a cloisonné
enamel altar vessel and contains leaves of
jade with berries of coral.

**Vase**
Qianlong reign (1736–1795)
Porcelain enamelled over the glaze in
'famille rose' colours; 35.5 x dia. 15.8 cm
Acquired by Lever before June 1907;
inv. no. LL 6060 (H 325)

This finely-potted vase, with its elegant
shape and carefully-arranged design of
peonies and a tree in blossom, is a good
example of the sophisticated wares
produced at this period for the Chinese
domestic market. It is in marked contrast to
the increasingly crowded decoration to be
found on contemporary export wares. On
the base is a Qianlong reign mark painted
in red enamel, its characters in the form
normally used on seals. Because the mark
refers to the reign during which the vase
was made, it is possible that it was
produced by an imperial factory.

**Glass picture**
Probably painted in Guangzhou
(Canton), Qianlong reign (1736–1795),
c.1760–80
*A shepherdess and falconer*
Painted and mirrored glass;
55.3 x 43.2 cm
Purchased by Lever, 1918;
inv. no. LL 8805 (X 2434)

Pictures of this sort, painted on the back of glass and then mirrored, were originally produced only for export to Europe. Because China itself could not produce glass of high enough quality, the glass panels were shipped there from Europe to be painted in the workshops of the Guangzhou area. Templates were used to produce series of nearly identical paintings. The pictures contain traditional Chinese features (in this example, the river and mountains as key elements in the landscape), but they are painted in a western manner heavily influenced by European prints sent to China for copying. The falconer and shepherdess figures reflect European ideas and fashions of the time, not Chinese taste: for wealthy Europeans, China was a fantastically exotic place and rural life was romantic and full of pleasure; for the Chinese, falconry and sheep-herding are barbaric activities associated with the nomads of the Mongolian grasslands. This painting appears to have retained its original carved and gilt Chinese frame.

# chapter 6

# Greek and Roman Antiquities

Lever became a serious collector of antiquities only after deciding to found the Lady Lever Art Gallery in June 1913; indeed only one item in the Gallery's collection, a Roman altar from the Capel-Cure sale of 1905, was purchased before that date. He probably formed the collection partly for didactic reasons: undoubtedly he saw an educational value in Classical art, for as early as the 1890s he had placed life-size photographs of Classical sculpture in the Port Sunlight schools (to which the Cheshire County Council objected, on account of the nudity, when they took over the schools in 1902–3). In the context of the Lady Lever Art Gallery, it seems likely that he was also concerned to show the prime sources for English neo-classical art, and especially for his collection of Wedgwood pottery.

Lever began acquiring antiquities within a month of the Gallery's inception, when he bought six Greek vases and a Roman bust at the Stafford House sale in July 1913 (see p. 59). Two years later he was a purchaser at the sales of Jeffery Whitehead (buying four Greek vases) and of C.T.D. Crews of Billingbear Park (five Greek vases and two Roman urns). But his two greatest opportunities both came in 1917. In that year he bought from the dealer Moss Harris twenty-seven vases and a few terracottas that had been in the collection of Alexander Ionides (1840–1898), which had already appeared at auction in both 1902 and 1912, before Lever became seriously interested in the field. He was also much the largest purchaser at Christie's sale of the collection originally formed by Thomas Hope (1769–1831), the most important group of antiquities to come on the market for generations. There Lever bought thirty-five ancient vases and sculptures, as well as the late 18th-century group of Cephalus and Aurora, which had been specially commissioned by Hope from John Flaxman when the latter was working in Rome (see p. 24).

Some at least of Ionides's collection was almost certainly acquired in Greece, which became a hunting-ground for antiquities during the 19th century. But at the time when Thomas Hope was collecting, almost all antique discoveries were excavated in Italy – Greek exports as well as indigenous Roman productions. Many of Hope's Greek vases were bought in 1801 from the second collection formed by Sir William Hamilton – as much of it as escaped destruction in the shipwreck of the *Colossus* on its journey to England – and it appears that all of these were Italian finds. Consequently, such vases were in the 18th century believed to be Etruscan in origin, and so this term became attached to the neo-classical style of painted decoration promoted by Robert Adam that was based on the decoration of Greek vases (see pp. 57, 98). The same misconception led Wedgwood to name his factory Etruria (see p. 72).

In fact some vases were manufactured in Italy, in the independent city-states founded by Greek colonists between the 8th and 6th centuries B.C.; but the artists, and their output, were still essentially Greek (see p. 97). However, the majority of painted vases were exported from mainland Greece – to Italy and the western Mediterranean initially, and later much further afield. At first Corinth dominated the trade, to be overtaken by Athens from about the mid-6th century.

Fig. 15 Antique and later sculpture displayed in the North Rotunda, *c.*1925

Most of the Gallery's Greek vases are decorated in the early, black-figure technique, which was adopted in Corinth in the early 7th century B.C., and in Athens by the 630s. The decoration is in black pigment applied to the red earthenware body, with the details of drapery etc. incised through the pigment to show up in red (see pp. 97–8). This technique was superseded in the late 6th century by red-figure decoration, in which the black pigment is applied to form the background, and the figures are left in reserve on the red body. The details are then painted in with a brush, and this allows for much freer drawing than is possible by the incised black-figure technique (p. 98).

The resulting more naturalistic treatment is a foretoken of the radically new approach in Greek art known as Classicism: a phenomenon that affected not only the visual arts, but tragedy and comedy, history and philosophy, all of which flourished in 5th-century Athens with the growth of democracy, and hence of an intellectual elite exercising freedom of thought and invention. It was driven by the will to confront the world in terms of man rather than the divine or supernatural. In the visual arts this meant the first ever attempt to represent the human figure from direct observation rather than by the use of conceptual formulae. But Classicism is also informed by a focus on design and proportion, a preoccupation in Greek art that goes back to the aptly named Geometric style of the 9th and 8th centuries B.C. The attempt to reconcile these two conflicting interests, in anatomical realism on the one hand, and rules of proportion on the other, gave rise to the naturalistic yet idealized treatment of the human – especially the male – form, that is quintessentially Classical.

This approach served as an inspiration to the art of Rome some five hundred years later, although the first formative Greek influence on Roman art was the Hellenistic tradition of the 3rd and 2nd centuries B.C. Hellenistic art had moved on in a number of ways from the Classical style of the 5th and 4th centuries – in the development of new techniques, in a wider variety of both style and subject-matter in sculpture, and in particular in a new emphasis on the individual and hence an incipient interest in portraiture (in both sculpture and painting). As the Greek cities of Italy and Sicily, and subsequently Greece too, were conquered by Rome in the 3rd and 2nd centuries, in artistic terms victory went the other way, and by the 1st century B.C. Rome itself had become a sophisticated and influential centre of late Hellenistic art; indeed most of the sculptors working in Rome were Greeks.

Yet Roman art was no mere pastiche of Hellenistic taste: it was shaped by a number of partly conflicting strands, not least a self-conscious revival of Classicism, when in the late Republic upper-class Romans began collecting Classical Greek sculpture, and also commissioning contemporary copies in Rome. At a lower social level the indigenous, so-called 'Plebeian' art of Republican Rome continued to thrive, a more austere idiom that valued content above style and certainly eschewed the elegance of Classicism. In the early Empire these two traditions were both influential on official as well as private art. The first Roman Emperor, Augustus (27 B.C.– 14 A.D.), favoured the Classical taste for ideological reasons: in attempting to rebuild a stable and responsible society after a century of turmoil, he encouraged art based on Classical simplicity and dignity as against the sumptuous late Hellenistic tradition, promoting an image of Rome as a new Athens and himself as its First Citizen, a new Pericles. But after Augustus's death the classicizing style declined into mannerism, while the 'Plebeian' taste gained increasing influence. At the same time a new style, both luxurious and grandiloquent, was created to fulfil the personal fantasies of some of Augustus's less level-headed successors. This style first found expression in the Golden House of Nero (Emperor 54–68 A.D.) – a fantastic, richly decorated, vaulted and apsed interior, built after the great fire of Rome in 64 A.D.: it is to this tradition that the three sculptures of the Flavian period (69–96 A.D.), seen here, belong (pp. 99–100). Classicism, however, enjoyed a last great flowering under the Emperor Hadrian (117–138), an intellectual and aesthete, who promoted the style for nostalgic and utopian rather than ideological reasons: a mood clearly felt in the figure of Antinous – commissioned by the Emperor himself – notwithstanding its 18th-century restorations (p. 101).

**Oinochoe (wine-pourer)**
Bearded Sphinx Painter
Etruscan ('Italo-Corinthian'), *c*.625–600 B.C.
Earthenware with black-figure decoration;
28.9 x 16.1 x dia. 15.6 cm
Purchased by Lever from the Ionides collection, 1917;
inv. no. LL 5063 (X 2253)

An oinochoe was used to dip into a bowl of wine to pour
out into cups. This one is decorated with a procession of
animals in two friezes: goats, boars, stags and lions (or
panthers). Though made in Etruria, it is of a type that was
strongly influenced in both form and decoration by vases
from Corinth, the most powerful of the trading Greek city-
states in the 7th century B.C. The hand responsible for the
best such 'Italo-Corinthian' vases, including this one, has
been named the 'Bearded Sphinx Painter'.

**Psykter**
Greek (Attic), *c*.525–500 B.C.
Earthenware with black-figure
decoration; 33.5 x dia. 25 cm
Purchased by Lever from the Hope
Heirlooms sale, 1917;
inv. no. LL 5034 (X 2138)

The vase is painted with a Dionysiac
revel: a dance of Maenads (the female
companions of Dionysus) being rudely
interrupted by lusty satyrs. The figure
on the donkey is probably Dionysus
himself, the god of wine and song. The
decoration is appropriate to this
vessel's function as a wine-cooler: wine
was placed in the psykter itself, which
in turn stood in a wide vessel filled
with ice or cold water. This shape was
only in fashion between about 525 and
475 B.C.

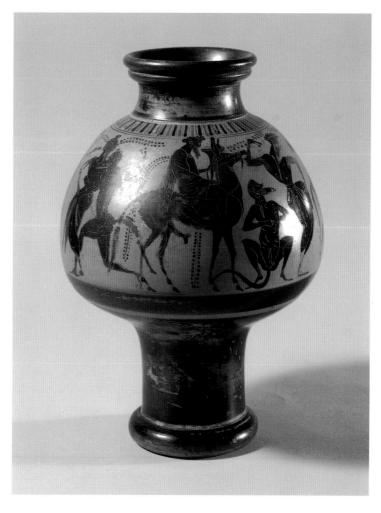

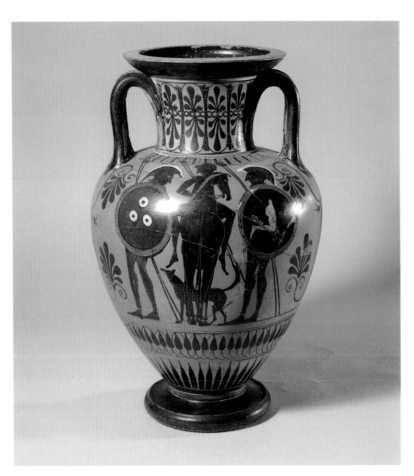

**Amphora**
Greek (Attic), c.510–500 B.C.
Earthenware with black-figure
decoration;
39.9 x dia. 26.2 cm
Purchased by Lever from the Hope
Heirlooms sale, 1917;
inv. no. LL 5014 (X 2120)

The central horse and rider are shown
in a boldly foreshortened head-on view,
with only their heads in profile,
between two standing warriors, one of
whom has turned away but is looking
back over his shoulder. The other side
of the vase has a scene, now badly
damaged, of Herakles (Hercules)
fighting three Amazons. The
ornamental motifs on this vase are
typical of the inspiration for late 18th-
century English neo-classical
decoration, especially the so-called
'Etruscan' style which was largely
derived from the publication of Sir
William Hamilton's first collection of
Greek vases.

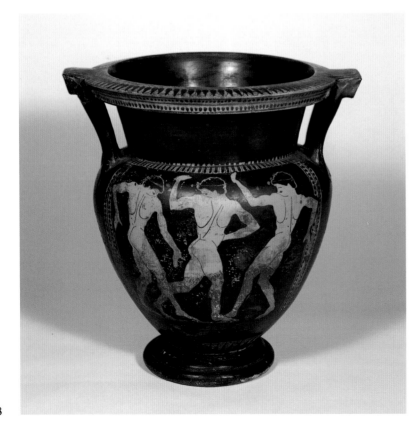

**Krater (mixing-bowl)**
Greek (Attic), c.500–475 B.C.
Earthenware with red-figure
decoration;
34.4 x 35.8 x dia. 31 cm
Purchased by Lever from the Hope
Heirlooms sale, 1917;
inv. no. LL 5035 (X 2139)

A krater was used for mixing wine and
water (wine was always drunk diluted).
This one shows the influence of Myson,
the leading painter of vases of this
'column-krater' shape, who signed (as
both potter and painter) a smaller
example found on the Acropolis at
Athens. This scene shows three
muscular dancing figures, all in
ambitious *contrapposto* poses (their
shoulders twisted away from their
hips), seen from behind with parts of
their faces hidden. They are probably
votaries of Dionysus who appears with
a satyr on the other side of the vase.
This vase is painted in the red-figure
technique that superseded black-figure
decoration in the late 6th century B.C. –
the black pigment now forming the
background with the figures left in
reserve on the red earthenware body
(see p. 95).

**Cinerarium (ash-chest)**
Roman, *c*.70–100 A.D.
Marble; 52.7 x 49.8 x 45.2 cm
Purchased by Lever from the
Hope Heirlooms sale, 1917;
inv. no. LL 11 (X 2161)

The inscription reveals that this urn was made for the ashes of Caius Perperna Geminus, who died at the age of sixty-eight, by his heirs Caius Perperna Agathopus, Saturnina and Fortunata, a freedman and two freedwomen. This panel and the surrounding harpies, birds and garland of fruit are largely antique. The urn was discovered in tombs in Siena in the early 18th century, but later belonged to the sculptor Bartolomeo Cavaceppi, who was probably responsible for the restorations – the lid, carved with reclining sphynxes, the base, with cornucopiae and flowers, and the ornament on the semicircular back. It was bought by Thomas Hope from Lord Bessborough in 1801.

**Candelabrum**
Roman, 1st century(?) A.D.,
restored in the 18th century
Marble; 246 x dia. 49 cm
Purchased by Lever from the Hope Heirlooms sale,
1917; inv. no. LL 16 (X 2157)

This candelabrum was extensively restored in the late
18th century, to satisfy contemporary taste for
'complete' works of art: the ancient elements on which
it is based – the main shaft below the ram's-heads and
part of the base – would not have been acceptable as
fragments. The restoration is very much in the style of
the sculptor and engraver Giambattista Piranesi
(1720–1778), but the history of this piece is unknown
before about 1804 when it was first recorded in
Thomas Hope's collection.

**Trapezophoros (table-support)**
Roman, *c.*100 A.D.
Marble; 118.6 x 50.6 x 37.8 cm
Purchased by Lever from the Hamilton Palace sale,
1919; inv. no. LL 8 (X 3732)

This table-support in the form of a lion monopodium
came from the collection of the Dukes of Hamilton at
Hamilton Palace. The base and the table-top itself are
mid-17th-century restorations. The Gallery has
another example of the same form, but in full-blown
baroque taste, which may have been made at the same
time as this antique example was restored; it too was
in the Hamilton Palace collection.

**Antinous**
Roman, *c*.130–138 A.D.
Marble; 232.5 x 69 x 91 cm
Purchased by Lever from the Hope Heirlooms
sale, 1917; inv. no. LL 208 (X 2170)

Antinous, a youth of renowned beauty from Bithynia in north-west
Asia Minor (Turkey), was the lover of the Emperor Hadrian, and was
deified after drowning himself in the Nile in 130 A.D. This statue, one
of many carved after his death, is based on a Classical Greek prototype
of the 5th century B.C. It was restored in the late 18th century by the
Roman sculptor Pierantoni, whose additions include the cup and the
jug; he has thus interpreted Antinous allegorically as Ganymede
offering ambrosia to Jupiter (or Hadrian).

# chapter 7

# The 'Museum' Collection

L ever's so-called 'Museum' collection comprises a number of disparate groups of material, listed together under this heading in the Gallery's original inventory apparently to distinguish them from his fine and decorative art collection. The principal components are ethnographic and Masonic items, although Greek and Roman antiquities (discussed in the previous chapter) were also inventoried mainly in this category, together with more recent archaeological finds (Lever's share from several digs that he helped to finance, principally in Egypt). It also includes several miscellaneous items, such as watches and sundials, keys, whips, constables' truncheons and whalebone staybusks, and other objects that do not easily fit into any of the categories of Lever's art collection.

The mainly ethnographic core of the 'Museum' collection has a longer history of public display than the Gallery's art collections, having been shown in the Lever Free Library and Museum, in Port Sunlight, from its opening in 1903. This material was transferred to Hulme Hall when that building was converted to a museum and art gallery in 1911, and was likewise originally intended to be prominently displayed at the Lady Lever Art Gallery, founded two years later. However, by 1922 when the Gallery displays were being finalized, constraints on space led to the total exclusion of the (now greatly enlarged) ethnographic collection, and much of it was sent to be exhibited at Lever Brothers' new London headquarters in Blackfriars. The Gallery retained a comparatively small part of the collection, mainly material from Africa and the south Pacific. After several years in storage this was loaned in the 1930s to other museums, and is now shown for the first time in this building, in the William Hesketh Lever Display (opened in 1996), where the full scope of Lever's activity as a collector is represented and examined.

Lever assembled most of his ethnographic collections during his business trips abroad, and he evidently associated them intimately with his commercial interests. They served partly as a symbolic link between his business and his philanthropic activities (which included the foundation of a model village like Port Sunlight in the Congo: see Fig. 16). The most ambitious of Lever's foreign travels were his three world tours of 1892–3, 1913–14 and 1923–4. In 1892 he landed briefly on Samoa where, as he noted in his diary, the inhabitants 'crowded round the ship in their canoes, offering for sale corals, shells, native cloth, pine apples, bananas, etc.', but he does not mention whether he made any purchases. On his second world tour, which he undertook shortly after deciding to build the Gallery (and very soon after the death of his wife), Lever made extensive acquisitions – including both the Japanese saddle and the North American drum (pp. 106–7) – which transformed his ethnographic holdings from a miscellany of curiosities into a collection of some importance. But by 1923 the greater part of this collection had been transferred to Blackfriars and other parts of his business empire, which were probably also the chief recipients of any new acquisitions made on his last world tour. After Lever's death some of the most important pieces, including two canoes from the Solomon Islands, were presented by the Gallery's Trustees to the British Museum.

Fig. 16 One of Lever's settlements in the Congo, probably Leverville, the model village he developed from 1911; photographed *c*.1924. (Unilever Information Services, Port Sunlight Heritage Centre)

Lever acquired his Masonic collection over a much shorter time-span in the 1920s, by making several purchases almost all from one collection, that of Albert Calvert (to which were later added Lever's personal regalia and a few items from other sources). His motives for doing so were again related to his business, for it was in that connection that he became involved with Freemasonry in the first place: in 1902 he was the first initiate of a new lodge bearing his name, established by some of his employees. He was rapidly promoted to high office at both local and national level (see Fig. 17), founded a number of lodges, and became a generous benefactor of Masonic charities. He saw Freemasonry as a useful tool to foster social cohesion and high standards of personal conduct among his male workforce, and the Masonic network he established at Port Sunlight deliberately reinforced the hierarchy within Lever Brothers itself, with separate lodges created for managers, supervisors and workers. Freemasonry was therefore an important instrument in Lever's paternalistic policy for the welfare of his employees. While the hierarchy he imposed was fundamentally alien to the Masonic ideal of equality among men, at that period of sharply defined class divisions it would have been socially accepted, not to say expected, in such an enclosed community as Port Sunlight.

Albert Calvert (1869–1946) was an unsuccessful and disreputable businessman and a prolific writer; he had a passionate interest in Freemasonry and probably began collecting Masonic relics soon after himself becoming a Mason in 1894. In his business career he set up a number of mining companies, none of which proved profitable, and by the end of the First World War the collapse of all his enterprises forced him to try to realize some of his assets. He wrote to Lever in November 1920 offering him his collection of Masonic items (mainly jewels and regalia) for £2,000, but readily accepted Lever's offer of £1,750. Over the next three years he offered Lever three smaller groups of Masonic relics, including a good collection of ceramics and glass and some important books and manuscripts, for a total price of £1,850: on each occasion Lever at first declined to purchase but eventually did so at a very substantial saving, paying £650 altogether for the three consignments. Calvert became desperate for cash at this time, for in 1922 he and an associate were convicted of fraud against a sister of the murdered Tsar Nicholas II, the Grand Duchess Xenia Alexandrovna, whom they had cheated into exchanging her jewels for shares in a worthless company making unusable printing machines (which were supposed to work by perpetual motion). Calvert was ordered to pay her £10,000 in reparations. While Lever was fully aware of Calvert's disgrace, he saw no grounds to doubt the authenticity of the items he had bought from him. His instincts were correct, for the collection he acquired by such economy of effort (as well as money) is of a scope and quality second only to that at Freemasons' Hall among public holdings of Masonic relics. Like the ethnography, this collection had been confined to storage for many years before the present showing in the William Hesketh Lever Display.

Fig. 17 George Hall Neale,
*William Hesketh Lever, Baron Leverhulme of Bolton-le-Moors, as Junior Grand Warden of England*, 1918
(Lady Lever Art Gallery, LL 3747)

**Masonic apron**
English, *c.*1760
Painted lambskin;
72 x 68 cm, plus ties 362 and 571 cm long
Purchased by Lever from the Calvert collection, 1923;
inv. no. LL 7653 (X 4691/16)

The earliest Freemasons' aprons were plain lambskins. The practice of decorating them, initially with simple drawing or painting, began in the 1750s, and this is a very early example of the type. Later examples were made of silk or satin, with very fine painted or embroidered decoration.

**Masonic punch-bowl**
Chinese, Qianlong reign, c.1780–90
Porcelain with under-glaze blue and over-glaze
enamels; 11.6 x dia. 28.9 cm
Purchased by Lever from the Calvert collection,
1922; inv. no. LL 7747 (X 4153/62)

This bowl, painted with Masonic emblems, was
made in China for the export market – a
flourishing 18th-century trade that ran parallel to
the trade in porcelain with armorial decoration: in
both cases the designs were copied in China from
engravings sent out from Europe. The decoration
of this bowl is mostly taken from designs used on
Masonic documents of the 1760s by Michael
Devon, clerk to the Grand Secretary of the premier
Grand Lodge of England from 1761 to 1777.

**Masonic jewel**
Thomas Harper (c.1735–1832)
English, hallmarked London 1807, altered c.1811
Silver; fully extended 13.2 x 6.6 cm
Purchased by Lever from the Calvert collection, 1920;
inv. no. LL 7512 (X 4078/2)

This unusual jewel belonged originally to J. Latrobe Wright,
member of an Irish Lodge at Waterford, who presented it in 1811 to
the actor Edmund Kean; it is the only evidence for the latter's
membership of Freemasonry. The original jewel of 1807 – a
remarkably late date for its rococo treatment – consists of a Master's
square and the crossed keys emblem of a Treasurer. The book was
added when Wright presented it to Kean. Calvert acquired this
jewel from the collection of the great actor-manager Sir Henry
Irving, also a Freemason.

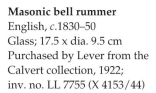

**Masonic bell rummer**
English, c.1830–50
Glass; 17.5 x dia. 9.5 cm
Purchased by Lever from the
Calvert collection, 1922;
inv. no. LL 7755 (X 4153/44)

This rummer, a type of large drinking glass, is
unusual both for its bell-shaped bowl (they
normally have straight tapering sides) and its
hour-glass stem, which recall 18th-century forms. It
is engraved with emblems representing both the
Craft (to which all Freemasons belong) and the
more exclusive Royal Arch order of Freemasonry.

## Saddle and harness
Japanese, 1812 and later
Lacquered and partly gilt hardwood, iron, iron inlaid with silver, painted and gilt leather, dyed hemp(?) string, gilt paper strip, basketry, wool, linen, silk;
H. from bottom of mud-guards to top of saddle (at front) 87 cm, W. of mud-guards 67 cm, H. from centre of crupper-cover to bottom of fringe 114 cm, W. of crupper-cover 61 cm
Purchased by Lever in Kobe, Japan, 1913; inv. nos. LL 8416–8423

This sort of harness was for ceremonial use rather than for battle. An inscription on the underside of the lacquered wood saddle records that it was made for a man called Fukugimi by Bangiko(?) Morifumi (from Ingebouri Prefecture, of Ise Province), and later restored by Sadafumi. A separate inscription gives the date 1812, probably referring to the initial date of manufacture rather than the restoration.
The large leather 'mud-guards' at either side of the saddle served also to protect the horse from chafing by the iron stirrups, which are inlaid with silver and of a distinctive Japanese form. The rest of the harness includes the wool bridle and iron bit, with two decorative tassels; a long looped wool strip, which may have been some form of breast-strap; and a wool crupper, secured to the saddle at either side and looped over the horse's tail to prevent the saddle sliding forwards; this would have been largely concealed by the 'crupper-cover', placed behind the saddle. The waisted gilt leather strap is a secondary (largely decorative) rein, to drape over the horse's neck in front of the saddle; the functional reins are missing.

**Drum**
North American (Western Great Lakes),
c.1880–1910
Painted wood, rawhide, cloth, beads, metal,
feathers; drum 22 x 58 x 55.5 cm,
support-stakes approx. 137 cm high,
drumsticks 34 and 35 cm long
Purchased by Lever from Mackay & Dippie of
Calgary, Canada, 1913; inv. nos. LL 8400–8406

The dance drum of the Ojibwa and other central Algonquian-speaking
tribes came into use in about 1880, partly in response to the new non-
nomadic life-style forced upon them after they were settled in
reservations. It was the focus of ceremonial dances performed by drum
societies, which were intended to promote peace. A new drum society
could be initiated by the gift of a drum from an existing society to
another community, and all claimed ultimate 'descent' from the
original drum made following a revelation to a prophetess of the Sioux
tribe. Ceremonies were held either in open-air enclosures or in circular
dance halls. The four ornamental support-stakes were secured in deep
holes in the ground (or in a specially made stand), so that the drum was
suspended much nearer to ground-level than shown here.

# Further Reading

Viscount Leverhulme,
*Viscount Leverhulme* (London, 1927)

W.P. Jolly,
*Lord Leverhulme, A Biography* (London, 1976)

Royal Academy, London,
*Lord Leverhulme*, ex. cat. (1980)

Edward Morris and Mark Evans,
*Lady Lever Art Gallery, Port Sunlight: Catalogue of Foreign Paintings, Drawings,
Miniatures, Tapestries, Post-Classical Sculpture and Prints* (Liverpool, 1983)

Geoffrey Waywell,
*The Lever and Hope Sculptures: Ancient Sculptures in the Lady Lever Art Gallery ... and
A Catalogue of the Ancient Sculptures formerly in the Hope Collection ...* (Berlin, 1986)

Martin Robertson,
*Greek, Etruscan and Roman Vases in the Lady Lever Art Gallery, Port Sunlight*
(Liverpool, 1987)

Mary Bennett,
*Artists of the Pre-Raphaelite Circle ... Catalogue of Works in the Walker Art Gallery,
Lady Lever Art Gallery and Sudley Art Gallery* (London, 1988)

Edward Hubbard and Michael Shippobottom,
*A Guide to Port Sunlight Village* (Liverpool, 1988)

Edward Morris (ed.),
*Art and Business in Edwardian England: The Making of the Lady Lever Art Gallery*,
reprinted from the *Journal of the History of Collections* Vol. 4, No. 2 (Oxford, 1992)

Xanthe Brooke,
*The Lady Lever Art Gallery: Catalogue of Embroideries* (Stroud, 1992)

Edward Morris,
*Victorian and Edwardian Paintings in the Lady Lever Art Gallery* (London, 1994)

Lucy Wood,
*The Lady Lever Art Gallery: Catalogue of Commodes* (London, 1994)

# Index